3/09

"Once again you will be encouraged and strengthened in your journey through the prolific pens of Quin Sherrer and Ruthanne Garlock, this time on a subject everyone has grappled with along the way: breaking bad habits. Using real-life stories from people in every walk of life, you will find in these pages tools to help you overcome areas in your own life that God wants to adjust."

—**Jane Hansen Hoyt**, president/CEO, Aglow International

"With wit and charm, the writing duo of Quin Sherrer and Ruthanne Garlock will disarm and free you with truth and light. From their years of experience in the Lord and in life, you will be given keys to unlock mysteries so you can truly live the abundant life Jesus promised all His followers. Warning: This book will set you free!"

—**James W. and Michal Ann Goll**, co-founders, Encounters Network; authors, *A Call to the Secret Place*, *God Encounters*, *Dream Language*, *Angelic Encounters* and many more

"We live in a day when fear, bitterness and temptation vie for our attention. It has never been more vital for each of us to have a vibrant, healthy God connection. *Lord, Help Me Break This Habit* is a practical, Spirit-breathed tool that brings healing to wounded or weak areas of your life. You will be positioned to overcome bad habits and unhealthy relationships and live free and fearless for your King. Quin Sherrer and Ruthanne Garlock are wise, time-tested mothers in the faith who have penned heaven's insights so you can experience life-transforming breakthrough!"

—**Lisa Bevere**, bestselling author and international speaker

"I was humbled to find myself on so many pages of this deeply wise book. Ruthanne and Quin aren't writing about evils that make headlines, but the 'household sins' we wrestle with daily. We can sometimes hide them from others, but never, the authors remind us, from God. The good news of this guidebook to freedom is that the same God who sees our failures will help us walk away from the old, self-defeating patterns. With a wealth of true stories, step-by-step guidance and pinpoint prayers, Ruthanne and Quin show us how."

—**Elizabeth Sherrill**, author, *All the Way to Heaven: Whatever You're Facing, Heaven Begins Now*

"Once again Quin and Ruthanne have married practical, easy-to-understand insights with relevant spiritual truths, and done so with a very challenging subject. Apply these principles and you really can be free from every debilitating habit!"

—**Dutch Sheets**, bestselling author, *Intercessory Prayer*; senior pastor, Freedom Church, Colorado Springs

"Congratulations to my special friends for a masterfully written and much needed book. Like Batman and Robin or Lucy and Ethel, Quin and Ruthanne have teamed up again to give hope and healing. These proven principles will help every area of your life. Indeed, true freedom is found only in Christ."

—**Rachel Burchfield**, president, Texas Bible Institute; co-pastor, Believer's World Outreach Church, Katy, TX

"It's one thing to be saved, but another thing to live free. *Lord, Help Me Break This Habit*, written by my friends Quin Sherrer and Ruthanne Garlock, is more than a book. It's a powerful tool. Read it carefully and you, too, will be able to graduate from the struggle to live freely (Romans 7) to the freedom of Christ as your very life (Romans 8)!"

—**Eddie Smith**, bestselling author and conference speaker

Lord,
Help Me
Break This
Habit

Lord,
Help Me
Break This
Habit

*You Can Be Free
from Doing the
Things You Hate*

Quin Sherrer
and Ruthanne Garlock

Chosen

a division of Baker Publishing Group
Grand Rapids, Michigan

Published by Chosen Books
A division of Baker Publishing Group
P.O. Box 6287, Grand Rapids, MI 49516-6287
www.chosenbooks.com

Printed in the United States of America

Library of Congress Cataloging-in-Publication Data
Sherrer, Quin.
    Lord, help me break this habit : you can be free from doing the things you
  hate / Quin Sherrer and Ruthanne Garlock.
       p. cm.
    Includes bibliographical references.
    ISBN 978-0-8007-9464-4 (pbk.)
    1. Habit breaking—Religious aspects—Christianity. I. Garlock, Ruthanne.
  II. Title.
BV4598.7.S54 2009
241′.3—dc22   2008040782

The circumstances of certain events and some names of persons and locations have been changed to protect individuals' privacy.

Contents

Acknowledgments

We wish to thank:

- Those who shared their inspiring testimonies in the pages of this book.
- Our faithful prayer partners who prayed diligently for us.
- Ann Spangler, our longtime friend and former agent, who has inspired us through many writing projects, including this one.
- Jane Campbell, editorial director, who has encouraged us in the development of this, our first release with Chosen Books.
- Trish Konieczny, our editor for this project, and all those at Baker Publishing Group who had a part in getting this book into your hands.

Quin: I am forever grateful to some special friends who were always available when I called for extra prayer: Fran Ewing, Mary Jo Pierce, JoAnne Bailey, Jane Droge, Martha Lucia,

Tommie Woods, Kerry Bruton, Mary Beth Pichotta, Judy Ball and Quinett Simmons. I am also greatly indebted to four special pastors who spoke into my life and influenced me in my spiritual walk over the years: Peter Lord, Forrest Mobley, Dutch Sheets and the late Jamie Buckingham.

Ruthanne: I wish to honor my mother, Hazel Sandidge, and my late husband, John, for the godly ways they influenced my life over the years. Also, I express great appreciation for the many friends and family members, near and far, who comprise my "prayer posse." These are the ones I know will pray when I call for counsel, comfort or prayer—and often they call or email me when they sense I may need an encouraging word. These God-ordained relationships continue to inspire my life every day.

Introduction

"Hey, when I became a Christian, I thought I'd be cleaned up—no more foul language or sexual lust or judging others— yet they have a foothold in my life," an old classmate told me just before I prayed for him as he lay in his hospital bed. He had been a Christian for some years, yet he still grappled with bad habits he did not want.

What is a habit? Webster defines it as "a behavior pattern acquired by frequent repetition."[1]

Maybe you, too, thought becoming a Christian would instantly free you of all your bad behavior patterns. Perhaps you learned this Scripture when you accepted Jesus as Savior:

> Therefore, if anyone is in Christ, he is a new creation; old things have passed away; behold, all things have become new.
>
> 2 Corinthians 5:17

Yet most of us discovered early on that the "become new" part is not instantaneous. The minute we confess, repent of our sin and seek God's forgiveness, we receive salvation and cleansing by the blood of Jesus. But the magnetic pull of worldly ways still entices us to stray from God's best for us.

We are all creatures of habit, and our habits profoundly affect who we are. First, we make our habits. Then our habits make or break us.

Sometimes we bring baggage with us when we become Christians—things we know are wrong, but cannot seem to unload. How do we get rid of those unwanted habits? That is what this book is about.

In these pages, you will read stories of people just like you who overcame many obstacles to shed their unrighteous ways simply by asking for God's help and empowerment, then following His direction. Some had to stop frequenting their old haunts. Others had to give up certain friends. Still others had to ask for or offer forgiveness. Most of them, though, were able to overcome their bad habits and begin walking out their newness in Christ.

If you desire to cast off your excess baggage and get free of bad habits that hold you back from God's best, the testimonies recounted here will encourage you. Whether you are struggling with criticism, anger, fear, worry, grief, addictions, gossip, impure thoughts or other sin patterns that hinder your walk with God, these stories will give you a new sense of hope.

You, too, can be victorious!

—Quin Sherrer

1

Why Do I Do the Things I Hate?

I don't really understand myself, for I want to do what is right, but I don't do it. Instead, I do what I hate. . . .Who will free me from this life that is dominated by sin and death? Thank God! The answer is in Jesus Christ our Lord.

Romans 7:15, 24–25, NLT

He [God] knows you can't solve the problem of an old sinful self by simply improving your behavior. He must change your nature, give you an entirely new self—the life of Christ in you—which is the grace you need to measure up to His standards.

—Neil Anderson[1]

A mother in Tennessee was so fed up with her thirteen-year-old daughter's bad behavior that she made her stand on a busy street in their city and wear a sign stating, "I don't obey my parents. I'm a liar. I steal from my mom. I have a bad attitude."

The teen told reporters that the embarrassing way she wore her offenses on a sign for passersby to see was eye-opening, and that she was going to start behaving better. Her mother declared her love for her daughter and said while other ways she had tried to get her daughter to change had not worked, she hoped this would.[2]

While none of us would want to publicly expose our own bad habits, things one friend called "household sins," we easily forget that God sees them anyway. But it is His desire to help us change—first inwardly, and then outwardly. Have you discovered that all the trying in the world will not change your bad habits or wrong behavior unless you do it in the context of trusting God, led by His Spirit?

Identifying Habits We Need to Quit

We are all creatures of habit. We all develop habits that affect who we are and how we view ourselves. Maybe you can identify with some of these people who are on the road to overcoming their weaknesses:

- Misplaced priorities: Ben worked from ten to sixteen hours a day because he considered his job such a high priority. Most of his children had left home by the time he made a commitment to Christ and realized he needed to change his work habits. "I was too strict on the kids when they were at home, and I spent too much time at the factory because I was 'production-oriented,'" he admits.

- Addicted to exercise: Deb spent four hours every weekday morning doing aerobics and bodybuilding, swimming or playing racquetball at the health club. Then she would go home for a long nap before preparing supper for her husband. Frequently, she met a relative for another racquetball game afterward. She wanted to feel good about herself, but one day she realized her exercise program controlled her life. *Why am I so driven to exercise?* she asked herself. *Is it for compliments or self-satisfaction? Or for my health's sake?* After asking God to show her a more balanced approach, she cut back on her hours at the club and is now a volunteer teacher who helps others improve their health.

- Pride and arrogance: Dick liked to impress his buddies with his intellect, letting them know he considered himself smarter than any of them. When relating any incident he had experienced, he stretched the truth so far it was simply unbelievable. In spite of Dick's years on the job, his boss finally fired him because of his rudeness to those working under him. Dick reevaluated his lifestyle, then read a book that made him contemplate the consequences of his behavior. Others recognized that he truly had changed when he stopped bragging, began speaking kindly and offered to help others. Finally, he landed a consulting job. By identifying his own self-deception and resolving to change, Dick is on the road to recovery.

- Angry at God: Though Theresa survived the surgery required to spare her life, she lost the baby she desperately wanted. Negative thinking took over, and routine daily tasks exhausted her. She snapped at her husband too often. One day a friend took her to the park for a heart-to-heart talk. "Usually there are three people we blame when life doesn't go according to our plans—ourselves, others and God," Lynne told her. "I think you're blaming Him for your loss." Handing Theresa a red helium balloon and a black marker, Lynne suggested she write a letter to God on the balloon, telling Him how she was feeling, and then release it. After some quiet moments alone, Theresa scribbled her hurts on the balloon until she had nothing more to say, then she let it go and watched as the red speck disappeared in the sky. Feeling a soothing calm and peace restored to her soul, she realized this was a healing moment in her grief journey.[3]

Making Right Choices

Yes, we do myriads of things we really hate. To name a few:

- criticism
- complaining
- worry
- pride
- envy
- anger
- gossip
- failure to forgive
- self-reliance
- failure to care for our bodies
- neglecting our families
- indulging in harmful habits

We know these attitudes and actions are wrong. Yet we often seem helpless to change. Which raises the question: "Why do we do the things we hate?" The Bible is our guidebook for finding answers.

When Adam and Eve sinned in the garden, they made an irreversible choice. God had given them only one restriction: They were not to eat from the tree of good and evil (see Genesis 2:15–17). But they listened to the voice of temptation and chose to disobey. Because all humankind has inherited their sinful nature, our natural tendency is to make wrong choices, too. However, from the beginning God had a plan to redeem us by sending Jesus to pay the penalty for our sins.

> Set a guard, O LORD, over my mouth; Keep watch over the door of my lips. Do not incline my heart to any evil thing, To practice wicked works With men who work iniquity.
>
> PSALM 141:3–4

Today, even after receiving Christ as our Savior, we daily face the choice of whether to follow God's ways or walk in our own. Sometimes we experience a struggle of conscience over doing what we know is right. Yet the more we learn about Jesus—who He is and what He has provided for us—the more we want to choose His ways and reflect His identity.

It is important to remember that we do not need to work to earn God's approval. He already loves and accepts us because He sees us as forgiven through the redemptive work of Christ. But yielding our will to His—allowing the Holy Spirit to guide and strengthen us in making right choices—pleases Him and makes for a more fruitful and contented life, as our next story illustrates.

Overcoming a Critical Nature

Peggy, a candid friend, shared with us about her effort to resist her habit of constantly criticizing other people. She held herself and everyone around her to a high standard of excellence. When others did not live up to that standard, she became annoyed and impatient, feeling she had to take up the slack for them.

"I was so busy keeping pace with a home, husband, three children and volunteer work, I seldom had time to enjoy life," she said. "Trying to follow up on everyone else's work to put things in apple-pie order, whether at home, at church or in my children's schools, exhausted me."

Acknowledging that being critical made her impatient with others and was not a godly attitude, Peggy resolved to resist this temptation. But the next thing she knew, it would surface again.

"I don't believe you like me," her husband commented one day as a result of her constant criticism.

"I married you, didn't I?" she snapped back.

Such exchanges were typical for Peggy until she came across a book on conflict resolution that suggested "open discussion" about the things that bother you. First you have to acknowledge that the problem may be in you, the author advised. You should not "dump on" or accuse another person, but in a calm manner talk to him or her about whatever issue is bothering you.[4]

"This worked well for me as I accepted the concept that you never really know another person unless you trust them with your inner feelings," Peggy said. "At home I began taking responsibility for my own negative reactions, calmly telling family members how I felt instead of nursing inner criticism."

For example, one day Peggy explained to her husband that when she waited for him and he did not show up, she felt the same panicky feeling she had experienced as a child when she got separated from her parents at the circus. Instead of the usual ranting at her husband's carelessness, Peggy took this quiet approach, which caused her husband to apologize for letting her down.

"When we began to communicate more openly, my family and I actually could laugh at our mistakes," she told us. "But I still needed to overcome my habit of judging and criticizing others outside our home. The lights went on when I heard a pastor explain that God makes a distinction between those who are spiritually immature and those who, like me, rebel against His teachings. I'd been a Christian for decades, but I still resisted the mandate, 'Do not judge.' "

> Let the words of my mouth and the meditation of my heart Be acceptable in Your sight, O LORD, my strength and my Redeemer.
>
> PSALM 19:14

Peggy knew she had experienced a breakthrough when she began to feel compassion for her fellow believers, accepting them at their level of spiritual growth. "It's very liberating not to always be criticizing others and trying to fix every problem," she concluded. "I just refuse to entertain those critical thoughts that still come knocking at the doorway of my mind, and I release other people to God."

I (Ruthanne) can identify with Peggy's struggle because God has dealt with me about the same problem. Years ago while visiting my mom, we were watching a Christian television program she regularly enjoyed. The speaker happened to be one I did not like, and toward the end of the program I made a cynical comment about the person. This is an example of how we so easily commit "household sins" when our guard is down—we are not "watching our p's and q's" because of being in familiar surroundings with people we are not trying to impress.

"Well, I try never to criticize anyone I think is doing more for God than I am," Mom said quietly.

Her words struck me to the core. My bad attitude was exposed, and I realized how arrogant and judgmental I was. After apologizing to her, I repented and asked the Lord to change my heart and help me stop being so critical of others.

Now, when tempted to criticize someone, I remember that visit, as well as another of Mom's admonitions: "If you can't say something good, then don't say anything at all."

No Complaining Allowed

A Midwestern pastor challenged members of his congregation to try to go 21 days without complaining, gossiping or being sarcastic. He had read that it takes 21 days to form a new habit, so he wondered whether participants could break old habits in the same time span. His goal was to see changed lives.

Those wishing to take part were given purple vinyl wristbands and a single rule: If you complained, gossiped or made a sarcastic comment, you had to switch the band to the other wrist and start over at day one. Ushers handed out hundreds of the wristbands, but two months later, only one person had met the challenge.

> No one can tame the tongue. It is restless and evil, full of deadly poison. Sometimes it praises our Lord and Father, and sometimes it curses those who have been made in the image of God. And so blessing and cursing come pouring out of the same mouth. Surely, my brothers and sisters, this is not right!
>
> JAMES 3:8–10, NLT

A teenage boy said at first he switched his bracelet from one wrist to the other and started over ten times a day, then seven times a day, then the switches got fewer until he made it a whole day without any negative talk.

A teacher reported, "Like many others, I felt that I was a positive person, definitely not a whiner. This challenge has opened my eyes."

One man said, "I'd complain about my weight, my sleep, my family, my friends, my pets, my house, the laundry, co-workers, neighbors, other people's pets, the weather, money, work, etc." This challenge helped him realize he was a habitual complainer.

Speaking for her whole family, a mother said, "Immediately we realized our conversations centered around sarcasm and criticizing others, as well as our own family members. We just quit talking for a day or two until we figured out ways to talk to each other that did not involve complaining."

One dropout admitted the challenge did not work for him. "You can't change inborn human nature," he concluded. "My mouth was speaking before my mind was in action," another woman reported. "Now I think before speaking, and sometimes I just say nothing."[5]

In Scripture, we see how God's people brought judgment upon themselves for doubting His promise and grumbling because they did not want to fight the giants in order to possess the Promised Land (see Numbers 14:26–29). Not only were the adults judged for their disobedience, but the example they set also caused some of their children forty years later to again complain about God's instructions (see Numbers 32:6–8, 14). Clearly, God considers complaining a serious offense!

Sandpaper People

Does it seem to you that God places sandpaper people in your life—those abrasive ones who bring out the very worst in you? A controlling, gossipy neighbor . . . a teacher with a grudge against your child . . . a boss who is out to ax you or your spouse . . . a relative who stirs up strife in your extended family . . . an unbearable co-worker. . . . The list goes on.

When we are "stoned" with words by persecutors including family, friends, strangers or enemies, we have a choice. We can decide to forgive them, release them from our judgment and resolve to pray for them. Or we can remain chained to them by our resentment and anger.

Joy had a hard decision to make concerning a man who constantly berated her son Don when he played basketball for the junior high team. Sitting in the parents' cheering section, she could not avoid hearing this man's derisive remarks. Whenever Don made the slightest mistake, the man would scream, "Hey, Don—Mr. Stupid—got brains in your feet, kid?"

Once, Joy's husband became so angry that he left the game, knowing if he stayed he would punch the man in the face. Finally, her husband stopped going to Don's games at all.

> Let all bitterness, wrath, anger, clamor, and evil speaking be put away from you, with all malice. And be kind to one another, tenderhearted, forgiving one another, even as God in Christ forgave you.
>
> EPHESIANS 4:31–32

"My son was being humiliated and my husband was angry—I could think of nothing to do but pray," Joy shared with me (Quin). "I remembered a Scripture verse that says we should bless those who curse us—and I felt that's what this man was doing. So I prayed, 'Lord, in the name of Jesus, I forgive that man. I ask You to bless him. Bless him real good, Lord. Just keep on blessing him. Amen.'"

The following weekend, Joy went alone to the out-of-town game. The man who always yelled at her son saw her. "Mind if I sit here?" he asked, turning into the row where she sat. "Other parents from our team will probably sit in this section, too."

Joy hesitated. *Let him sit beside me?* she thought. *Is he serious?* Then she remembered her prayer. "Go ahead," she answered.

As the game progressed, Joy noticed the man was acting quite differently. Only once did he let go with a string of critical remarks about Don's performance. Turning to Joy, he said, "Oh, I'm sorry. I've got to learn to keep my mouth shut and control my temper."

This man she had prayed for and asked God to bless was now apologizing for yelling at her son! And that was the end of him spoiling the games for Joy.

"When Jesus taught us to bless those who persecute us, He knew it was to bring about a change—both in us and in them," Joy said. "The man eventually stopped yelling at any of the players and was always friendly to me at games."

Workaholics Need New Priorities

Workaholics have been called "the stereotype of modern life." Though not many people will admit to being workaholics, they are found in all job categories. When one's devotion to career becomes exaggerated, both the worker and his or her family suffer. Richard is one of the few businessmen we know who acknowledges his roller-coaster ride from being a chronic workaholic to finding balance in his priorities. He tells his story:

After finishing college in three years, I immediately started a business that required eighty-hour workweeks. I was in debt big-time and stressed to the max. My wife felt abandoned and lonely in a new town with no friends, no money and no husband to spend time with her.

Within a few years, I realized I might lose my marriage if I didn't cut back, so I sold the business. But two years later, I started another business and fell back into the same rut of long hours and high stress, a cycle I repeated several times. Like a drug addiction needing to be fed, my desire to be as successful as possible drove me to continue my quest for more.

When I had any spare time, I poured it into my church life. Before long, I was working less at the office but volunteering more at church. I tried to achieve balance but always got pulled back into overcommitting and overworking. I excused my behavior, reasoning that I was a hardworking Christian achieving worldly success while balancing my service at church.

I now realize I was striving to win the approval of my parents, friends and peers. Sadly, I was blind to the effect my behavior was having on my marriage and family. I did achieve what I set out to do for my family financially, and we reached a high standard of living—but at what cost? My wife would have preferred me to provide less financial success and more quality time for her and our children.

> There is therefore now no condemnation to those who are in Christ Jesus, who do not walk according to the flesh, but according to the Spirit. . . . For those who live according to the flesh set their minds on the things of the flesh, but those who live according to the Spirit, the things of the Spirit.
>
> ROMANS 8:1, 5

I'm not sure where we would be today had I not had a near-death experience while on a missions trip overseas. While lying with pneumonia in a dirty hospital in a third world country, my life flashed before me. Acknowledging that much of what I was working for was self-centered and insignificant to God, I promised I'd change things if He let me live. Due to several miracles in answer to prayer, I did live, and I did modify my lifestyle.

I sold businesses, cut my work schedule, reduced my number of employees by 90 percent and kept only one small family business. However, with all the newfound free time, I again got pulled into working too much at church and even went on staff full-time. I seemed to know only one speed—overdrive. This led to a repeat of all the things I was trying to escape, but again I used the excuse that I was doing it for God.

A few years of this affected my health, and I realized my "modifications" were not enough. Determined to change, I took off a few months to seek the Lord for His direction. Because of my tendency to overdo and overwork, I now refuse to say yes to requests without running them by my wife and getting her counsel. I can't say I have achieved perfection, but I'm making great progress.

Having drive and working hard for your family are good in themselves, but anything taken to extreme is dangerous. We can't see our blind spots—which is why they're called blind spots. And we're not good at judging for ourselves whether or not we have a well-balanced approach to work. We need to listen to family members and loved ones, then trust God to help us make wise decisions. Now that I'm at a better place of balance, I don't ever want to go back to where I was.

Today Richard is deeply involved in church missions projects that take him around the world. He has sold a major interest in his business to his son and tries to let him manage it without interference. He still works at the large city church where he was a founding elder, but he keeps limited hours. His favorite pastime is babysitting his grandchildren and enjoying time with them and his wife.

Achieving Self-Control

So how can we overcome our bad habits? One great suggestion we heard is to remember the four R's: respect for God, respect for self, respect for others and responsibility for our actions. Different people shared with us some of the ways they are learning to control their bad habits as they depend upon God's help:

- When tempted to make a wrong choice, I've learned to listen to the promptings of the Holy Spirit. Then I pray for strength not to engage in that negative behavior (see John 16:13; Romans 8:14).

- I search the Bible for a verse that deals with the habit I'm struggling with, then I commit the verse to memory. To make wise choices, I must determine to line up with the spirit of the Word.

25

- I continue to work at developing self-discipline, which for me means getting involved with a Christian support group and daily spending time in Bible reading and prayer.

Oswald Chambers gives us this valuable perspective on the purpose of prayer:

As long as you think you are self-sufficient, you do not need to ask God for anything. To say that "Prayer changes things" is not as close to the truth as saying, "Prayer changes *me* and then I change things." God has established things so that prayer, on the basis of redemption, changes the way a person looks at things. Prayer is not a matter of changing things externally, but one of working miracles in a person's inner nature.[6]

Perhaps the greatest step we can take toward changing our habits is simply to admit our need to change, then to rely on God's help to follow through. This enables us to throw off our guilt and experience His love and acceptance at a deeper level, which we discuss more in the next chapter.

PRAYER

Lord, help me recognize my unhealthy habits and move toward spiritual and physical wholeness. I truly want to please You and become the person You created me to be. Help me yield to the Holy Spirit's work in my heart to guide me through this process. I ask this in Jesus' name and thank You in advance. Amen.

2

Lord, I Need to Know You Accept Me

What then shall we say to these things? If God is for us, who can be against us?

Romans 8:31

God loves each one of us as if there were only one of us.

—St. Augustine[1]

Have you ever felt God did not love or accept you? Most of us have. Often we develop a subtle mindset that we are not good enough to receive God's love. Those who have suffered emotional trauma or abuse are especially vulnerable to being trapped by a sense of false guilt, false shame, inferiority or unworthiness.

God wants to set us free from these negative attitudes so we are able to freely receive His love, acceptance and promises.

Then the Holy Spirit can help us to deal with detrimental habits in our lives and begin seeing ourselves as God sees us.

Mary, a West Coast grandmother, experienced firsthand the explosive mix of abuse, alcohol and anger shortly after she married as a teenager. Her husband, Ted, was jealous and possessive, heaping cruelty upon her for most of their 46 years of marriage.

Why did Mary stay? She did not see leaving as a possibility. *How can I make it on my own financially?* she would ask herself. *Besides, my children need a dad,* she reasoned.

Sadly, her church's teaching that divorce was absolutely wrong and that a wife should submit to her husband helped keep Mary in a harmful relationship for far too long. Hers is a story we have heard from other women trapped in similar situations. Seeing no hope and no way out, they endure emotional, physical and sexual abuse. But this definitely is not God's plan for marriage! Mary tells us her story:

"We had a nice home, looked like a nice family and most people never knew how he treated me behind closed doors," Mary told me (Quin). "Ted's abusive words wounded my spirit and hurt almost as much as the beatings I endured from him when he was drinking."

When Ted would hit her or throw things at her, she would run and hide. Often he would shout, "It's your fault—you cause me to treat you this way!" Other times after he mistreated her, he would apologize.

"I'd have compassion for him and hope that maybe this time he really meant it," Mary said. "But I actually was in denial of what Ted was doing to me. Had it not been for the comfort of the Holy Spirit and God's words of consolation to me in Scripture, I couldn't have endured all the pain and heartache."

Then Mary got sick. Doctors said she had a rare kind of tumor at the base of her brain, causing her pituitary gland to produce ten times the normal amount of cortisol. Her weight soared, and she was also going blind, had arthritis, diabetes and osteoporosis, and was covered with skin blotches that made her look ninety years old.

"Ted treated me fairly well during my illness because the crisis scared him," Mary reported. "I had two surgeries and spent two years in intense physical therapy with a trainer to get my body back in shape. I lost a lot of weight, and eventually all my sicknesses disappeared. The doctor who said I had less than three months to live at the time of my diagnosis now declared I was 100 percent well!"

> Yet in all these things we are more than conquerors through Him who loved us. For I am persuaded that neither death nor life, nor angels nor principalities nor powers, nor things present nor things to come, nor height nor depth, nor any other created thing, shall be able to separate us from the love of God which is in Christ Jesus our Lord.
>
> ROMANS 8:37–39

When Mary was almost fully recovered, Ted began his abuse again. But by now she had begun working from her home, then got a job downtown—her first steps toward becoming independent.

One summer day while in a drunken stupor, Ted held Mary captive in a room for two hours, and she feared for her life. Fumbling for the cell phone behind her, she managed to keep her hands behind her back and dial 9-1-1. After the police arrived and took Ted away, Mary moved out for her own safety, but she could not bring herself to file charges against him.

She rented a secluded home and hid out for about seven months. Then a professional counselor helped her sort out her life issues. The counselor asked Mary one question that changed the course of her life: "What does God feel when one of His own is hurt?"

Mary knew in her heart that God did not desire her to be an abuse victim any longer. After two years of separation,

29

she realized Ted was not willing to change and finally filed for divorce.

"A pastor helped me see God loved me and wanted His best for me," Mary said. "I became active in church and prayer groups and began to recognize that I'm a person of worth. Ted's abuse had often made me feel I was worthless, but God helped me to fully forgive him. Today I own my home, still hold a job and walk about four miles every evening to keep in shape. I have no animosity toward Ted, because God has healed me from the pain he inflicted. When our grandchildren have special events, Ted and I are sometimes both there at the same time, and we're on friendly terms. My life is proof that God truly can change a person's heart."

Ted is in poor health and still drinks, but Mary is no longer afraid of him. She stands on God's Word and believes God will do what He says. One of her lifeline verses is Proverbs 3:5–6: "Trust in the LORD with all your heart; do not depend on your own understanding. Seek his will in all you do, and he will show you which path to take" (NLT).

In Mary's case we see how, over time, the Holy Spirit helped her see herself as worthy, loved and able to overcome. Such a long struggle also may occur when a person has suffered false accusations from a pastor or leader. This actually amounts to spiritual abuse, which can cripple a person for life unless he or she receives ministry and counseling. A friend who suffered shame and doubt for many years shares her story.

Accusations Breed Doubt

Doreen and her friends, most of them young believers in their twenties, often met in homes for worship and fellowship. One evening during one of their meetings, Doreen lay on the floor, prostrating herself in God's holy presence. It was a powerful time of worship for her. A pastor from Europe and her own pastor were there also.

The next day, Doreen's pastor asked if he could talk to her. When he came by, he told her the visiting pastor had sensed that she was a lesbian. Her pastor asked if it was true. "No, absolutely not!" Doreen insisted. "There is no inclination in me in that direction—it's simply not true."

Because her pastor was the spiritual authority over her, his words wounded her deeply. Yet he offered no apology, no prayer and no opportunity for counseling. And when gossip began spreading that she had lesbian inclinations, her pastor did nothing to stop the rumor.

For several years, Doreen continued to suppress her deep emotional pain. Because of the accusation, the power of suggestion was at work in her mind. *Does anyone else see me like this?* she wondered, while trying to do everything she could to prevent the lie from coming up again. She chose more feminine clothes, wore earrings, heels, bright colors—anything to keep from looking masculine.

> The Spirit Himself bears witness with our spirit that we are children of God, and if children, then heirs—heirs of God and joint heirs with Christ.
> ROMANS 8:16–17

Due to a job transfer, she relocated to another city and found a new church home. Still, plaguing doubts sometimes surfaced, and Doreen questioned, *Does God accept me as I am?* She continued pushing such thoughts down into the dark recesses of her soul. But finally, almost twenty years after she had been falsely accused, she went through a Christian counseling program.

Her counselor helped Doreen see that the words spoken against her had robbed her of many things, including her true identity in Christ. She had isolated herself from others, fearing that to get close to someone would again bring false accusations. The false rumor that her pastor did nothing to stop had caused her even to question God's love for her.

Doreen found freedom through renewing her mind with Scripture and memorizing verses from the Bible about who she is as a child of God. Today she has a fulfilling position in the company she has worked for since college, and she owns a beautiful home. In her spare time, she operates a website for a Christian ministry and finds great satisfaction in volunteering her skills. Now, at last, she is very sure the Lord loves her and accepts her as she is.

Do Not Compare Yourself with Others

While the Bible declares that we are fearfully and wonderfully made and that God fashioned our days (see Psalm 139:14–16), many of us are not satisfied with the way He created us. We just cannot stop comparing ourselves with others or even daydreaming about ways to appear more attractive—even if it means taking drastic measures.

Sarah was an insecure wife who thought cosmetic surgery would make her more appealing to her wealthy husband, Nick. She shares in her own words the consequences of her decision:

Stunned and dizzy, I couldn't believe the report from my mammogram: "A leak in the implant in your left breast has been detected. Surgery is recommended immediately."

I'd been sick for a long time, going from doctor to doctor trying to find the cause for my debilitating fatigue, aching muscles and joints, recurrent infections, digestive problems and mental fog. Friends and family members prayed for my healing as I sought treatment for the symptoms without getting a specific diagnosis.

Twenty-four years earlier, I'd decided to have breast augmentation, hoping to become more attractive to my husband. *If Nick finds me more desirable, then surely he'll love me and want to be with me,* I thought at the time. We were having marital problems, and deep down I hadn't wanted to go through with it. When I approached Nick about the possibility of surgery, I wanted him to say, "I love you just the way you are; you don't need to change anything." Instead he said, "Do whatever you want to do—I don't care."

I didn't know at the time that he was having affairs with other women. Nick's wandering eye, verbal abuse and constant criticism of me only reinforced the feeling I'd had since childhood that I didn't measure up. I believed that surely the problems in our relationship must be my fault.

> As the Father loved Me, I also have loved you; abide in My love. . . .You did not choose Me, but I chose you and appointed you that you should go and bear fruit, and that your fruit should remain, that whatever you ask the Father in My name He may give you.
>
> John 15:9, 16

Though a Christian at the time, I failed to seek direction from the Father who loves me unconditionally. Feeling insecure and desperate to hold my marriage together, I agreed to the surgery. I've heard it said that what you compromise to keep, you lose. My life is proof of that statement. I attempted to provide a shortcut solution to my spiritual, emotional and relational problems by changing my physical appearance. But the plan failed, and ten years later my marriage ended. The Bible says, "There is a way that seems right to a man, but in the end it leads to death" (Proverbs 14:12, NIV).

God led me to a wonderful Christian counselor who helped me face my insecurities, grow up emotionally and learn to depend on the Lord for the love I needed. Then I moved to a new town and, in God's time, met a wonderful Christian man. We are happily married and are very much in love today.

As my health worsened and my energy waned, I blamed the problems on hormones, menopause or aging—never on the silicone implants, as I'd been assured they were safe. Now, with the test results before me, I knew my immune system was compromised. After research and prayer for God's help and direction, He led me to a surgeon in Atlanta, six hours away. She also had suffered from leaking silicone breast implants and had developed a protocol for treatment through surgery, followed by natural supplements and whole foods. Two weeks later, I had the implants removed.

Today I count myself blessed. Though I have physical scars, I've learned to put my confidence in the God who made me and loves me as I am. My strength and energy are returning, and my husband continually encourages me. But I have a burden for other women who suffer as I did.

Too many women who have received silicone breast implants are still sick—often misdiagnosed or told that nothing is medically wrong. Since most doctors are not taught about the symptoms of silicone poisoning or its relationship to autoimmune and neurological diseases, they fail to recognize the root cause of the problem.

Because I've been transparent about my own struggle, women who are suffering from low self-esteem, silicone poisoning or both often call me for advice. I just share my experience and try not to make anyone feel guilty. But I do recommend that each person balance the benefits of cosmetic surgery against the risks, then seek God's guidance before making a decision.

We realize not everyone can identify with Sarah's experience. But most of us have faced personal challenges at one time or another when we failed to see ourselves as God sees us.

No Longer a Victim

Have you ever felt weighed down with a blanket of shame you just could not seem to shake off? Judith struggled with this for years, until she discovered the underlying cause of it.

"I felt oppressed by something, but I didn't know what it was," Judith wrote in response to reading one of our previous books. "Now I'm being set free from unhealthy, toxic shame. The Lord showed me I was stuck behind my inability to receive love. I never really believed anyone, including my husband, when they said they loved me."

Like scores of women we have met, Judith grew up in a family with an alcoholic father. His drinking and angry rages, contrasted with his perfectionism and unreasonable demands, marked her with shame.

> Through Jesus the forgiveness of sins is proclaimed to you. Through him [Jesus] everyone who believes is justified from everything you could not be justified from by the law of Moses.
>
> Acts 13:38–39, NIV

"I'm beginning to realize, as the Holy Spirit brings it to light, that my shame was not for what I did or didn't do, but for who I was," she said. "Because of the way my father treated me, I felt I was never perfect enough, educated enough, pretty enough, smart enough or talented enough. The rejection and oppressive guilt caused me to be double minded.

"I read somewhere, 'Don't try to get in touch with your feelings; get in touch with truth and your feelings will change.' Now, when I hear shame trying to rule, I hear the Holy Spirit say, *No shame! No shame!* I could never earn God's love, but I cannot be separated from His love. The verse that's true for me is, 'He heals the brokenhearted and binds up their wounds [curing their pains and their sorrows]'" (Psalm 147:3, AMP).

We want you to see that you are not a hopeless victim. You can be free from the prison of shame, even though you may believe it is impossible to change the way you feel and the way you perceive yourself. Freedom is available if you cooperate with God. These are five helpful steps you can take toward becoming free:

1. Begin to see yourself as God sees you, based on Scripture. Ask Him to reveal this truth to you, and learn self-esteem from within.
2. Establish healthy boundaries. Do not allow anyone to violate your body or your self-esteem. As you begin to respect yourself and see yourself as God sees you, your demeanor will command the respect of others.
3. Get to know yourself and your personality, then discover your talents and exercise them. Show respect for your body by establishing good grooming and health habits. Take the risk of learning who you can trust as your friends and how to respond to others socially.
4. Work toward becoming interdependent with other people in your life. Do not isolate yourself, yet do not be helplessly dependent on others (see 1 Corinthians 12:21–27).
5. Do life moderately—that is, strike a balance between emotional highs and plunges into depression. Allow yourself to make mistakes and learn from them without presuming you are a bad person because of a blunder.[2]

How Do You See Yourself?

As Judith's experience illustrates, shame has to do with how we feel about ourselves. However, guilt feelings result from our behavior. When we have done something wrong, our consciences cause us to feel at fault. Perhaps because of your upbringing, you have a supersensitive conscience, which produces guilt feelings about relatively minor matters. Or you may have a hardened conscience because of repeated wrongdoing. Scripture tells us, "To the pure, all things are pure, but to those who are corrupted and do not believe, nothing is pure. In fact, both their minds and consciences are corrupted" (Titus 1:15, NIV).

All of us have experienced feelings of remorse over wrong actions or feelings of regret when we failed to speak or act as we should. Although we cannot go back and do things differently, we can confess, repent and ask God for forgiveness. Not only is His grace freely available, but He is able to redeem our mistakes in amazing ways. The Bible is full of imperfect people just like us, and their stories should give us confidence that no situation is beyond God's ability to restore.

The distortion in some people's self-perception comes because they put themselves at the center of life rather than putting God in that place. Dr. Diane Langberg comments on this:

> Some of us have made ourselves central by investing all our energies into thinking how *important* we are. We are proud and arrogant and are devoted to caring for ourselves at the expense of others. Others of us have made ourselves central by investing our energies into *hating* ourselves. We treat ourselves in ways that are unfounded. Our minds are continually focused on how bad, unimportant and worthless we are. Both extremes are wrong, yet one or the other may be constantly pulling us in its direction. . . . We can be redeemed in Christ. God has intervened so as to again make us look like Him.[3]

She points us to the Scripture, "But we all, with unveiled face, beholding as in a mirror the glory of the Lord, are being transformed into the same image" (2 Corinthians 3:18).

"This transformation is not instantaneous, it is a process," Dr. Langberg explains. "It is important to understand that our reshaping and redefining continues lifelong. Our acceptance by God in Christ is complete because it was bought and paid for in full at His cross."[4]

No Inferiority Allowed

"We have to get rid of our 'stinking thinking' and accept the fact that God loves us unconditionally, just the way He made us," one friend of ours often comments.

Because we belong to God, He helps us bring balance and order to our lives. Part of our wrong thinking occurs when we allow what other people say or think about us to limit us in reaching our full potential. We wallow in inferiority.

Years ago I (Quin) read an article that indicated 90 percent of us feel second-rate when we compare ourselves with others. Of course, there is no way to prove that. But too many people suffer from an inferiority complex because they believe other people are better than they are—whether in looks, skills or circumstances. Sometimes you encounter someone who gives the impression that he or she is superior to others, but many times that is just a façade to cover his or her inner feelings of inadequacy.

> He saved us, not because of righteous things we had done, but because of his mercy. He saved us through the washing of rebirth and renewal by the Holy Spirit, whom he poured out on us generously through Jesus Christ our Savior, so that, having been justified by his grace, we might become heirs having the hope of eternal life.
>
> Titus 3:5–7, NIV

The little girl who is constantly told by her dad, "You are a beautiful, precious princess," grows up with a great self-image. But if the "prince" she marries begins treating her like the ugly stepsister, often she embraces that negative message and plunges into a sea of inferiority. Overcoming such an inferiority complex is possible—but only when you stop focusing on your own mind's image of yourself that is not necessarily true and change how you perceive yourself. Here are a few examples of people who had to overcome inferiority:

- Debbie, who always struggled with weight problems, would not look people in the eye because she felt fat. When she was an adult, she became a Christian and sought counseling to get free. She admitted that as a child, whenever her family drove past the neighbor's pig farm, her mother would laugh and say, "Look, there are a lot of Debbies out there." Her mother's words kept Debbie from accepting her true worth.

- Because Gilbert made poor grades in school, his dad told him he would never amount to anything. He believed that lie, so he never applied to a college or even a vocational school. He settled into a job felling trees, which he hated. Yet he read a lot and became knowledgeable in several fields. One day his pastor challenged him to see himself as God created him and to become more people-oriented. Today he has a computer job in a large office, and he thoroughly enjoys it. He also helps people in his church who suffer the same feelings of unworthiness that once plagued him.

- Christy grew up in a home filled with arguing, name-calling, fighting and sexual abuse. When she was eight and told her father she wanted to be in a beauty pageant someday, he laughed and said if anyone in the family ever entered one, it would be her prettier younger sister. Christy got the message—"you're not worth anything"—and her behavior mirrored that rejection through most of her life. Finally, an aunt led her to Christ, and she was set free through Christian counseling.

- Daryl, who was underweight, with his face pocked from acne, suffered being called names such as "Beanpole," "Scarface" or "Lightweight." He took up wrestling to try to overcome his poor self-image, but he was not good at it. Only after he moved away from his hometown and started attending a new church did he realize he had allowed other people's opinions to shape his self-image. Thankfully, he sought help and came to see himself for who God created him to be.

The primary key to overcoming an inferiority complex is simply to accept yourself for who you are and cease comparing yourself to others. That does not mean you do not need to get rid of wrong habits, attitudes and feelings. But when you recognize your own uniqueness, then the Holy Spirit can bring healing to the wounded areas in your life and help you develop into the person God intended all along. Every person is God's individual creation, and each of us will always be unique in His eyes.

The Bible says, "We are His workmanship, created in Christ Jesus for good works, which God prepared beforehand that we should walk in them" (Ephesians 2:10). *Workmanship* here means "that which is manufactured, designed by an artisan."[5] The Master Designer created us as His handiwork. Dare we refuse to accept ourselves as He designed us?

The Christian's Position

We need to know our position in Christ. He redeemed us through shedding His blood, thereby delivering us from the power of darkness and transferring us into the Kingdom of the Son (see Colossians 1:13–14). You might want to memorize some of the following verses and make it a habit to declare them regularly to remind yourself of who you are in Him.

- I am a child of God (see Romans 8:15–16; Galatians 3:26; 4:6).
- I am no longer condemned (see Romans 8:1).
- I am an heir to God's Kingdom (see Galatians 3:26; Romans 8:17; Titus 3:7).
- I am salt and light (see Matthew 5:13–14).
- I am chosen (see John 15:16).
- I am a dwelling place of God (see 1 Corinthians 3:16; 6:19).
- I am a member of the holy priesthood (see 1 Peter 2:4–5).
- I am forgiven (see Ephesians 1:7).
- I am gifted, with a strategic position in the Kingdom (see Romans 12:5–6).
- I am called (see Ephesians 4:1).
- I am a friend of Christ (see John 15:14).
- I am holy and blameless (see Ephesians 1:4).
- I am God's workmanship (see Ephesians 2:10).[6]

We no longer need to remain burdened by a sense of false guilt, false shame, inferiority or unworthiness. God desires to fulfill His purpose for each one of us individually and to conform us to the image of His Son.

Now let's turn our attention in the next chapter toward another challenge we may need to face—trying to stay calm when conflict and chaos are raging all around us.

PRAYER

Thank You, Jesus, for laying down Your life as a sin offering for me. Thank You that whenever I sin and am burdened by guilt, I need only come to You with true repentance to be cleansed by the precious blood You shed for us. Help me to continue walking in Your freedom. Thank You that I'm Your workmanship, created for good works. I choose, through the power of the Holy Spirit, to live in accordance with God's description of me as presented in His Word. Amen.

3

Lord, Help Me Stay Calm

If you are angry, don't sin by nursing your grudge. Don't let the sun go down with you still angry—get over it quickly; for when you are angry you give a mighty foothold to the devil.

Ephesians 4:26–27, TLB

I have a small sign above my desk which says: "You are fast becoming what you are going to be." . . . If I let my anger remain, if I grow satisfied with it, or if I become resigned to my depression—then I will become that in the future. Every six months we need to sit down with paper and pen and list all the attitudes we exhibit when we are criticized. Then on the other side we should list all the attitudes we ought to exhibit.

—Jamie Buckingham[1]

Staying calm when everything is going well is one thing—but keeping your cool under the pressure of conflict, disappointment or trauma is quite a different matter.

Self-control, one of the fruits of the Spirit, is a characteristic most of us want to exhibit in our lives. But only by cooperating with the Holy Spirit's work in us can we cultivate this fruit. What comes to mind when you think of anger? Being out of control? Feeling irritable? Having a temper tantrum? Flying into a rage? Having a bad attitude? Being annoyed? Actually, all these apply.

Our emotions, including anger, are God-given and therefore are not sinful. When we fail to deal properly with our anger, disappointment or grief in scriptural ways, though, these emotions soon negatively affect our behavior. We find freedom when we face the problem, repent for allowing our feelings to control us and receive God's peace. Then as we yield to His ways, the Holy Spirit can help us express our emotions in appropriate ways.

Losing Control

If you tend to become angry easily, do not be surprised if your anger surfaces in ways you will later regret. Such was the case with Floyd, who found out the hard way that he needed God's conviction and help to keep his temper under control. He tells us his story:

I was a substitute science teacher for the last two periods of school at a junior high. For some reason, on one particular day the fourth-period class of eighth graders was unruly, hyperactive and uncontrollable. Everything I did to get them to settle down failed.

"Class, be quiet and pay attention!" I yelled at them, losing my temper. They kept up their chatter and laughter, so I shouted again, "You are unruly and disrespectful—now shut up! I'm going to report each of you to your teacher." Still they didn't calm down. You'd think a demonic spirit had been unleashed in this classroom.

The next class, full of seventh graders, was almost as bad. I yelled and screamed at them, too, certainly not a right way to get them to listen. Before leaving that day, I wrote a letter to the teacher telling her what had happened and that I wouldn't serve as a substitute teacher for those two classes again.

I remembered my wife's words to me once: "Floyd, if you don't learn to control your anger at home, it's going to show up and embarrass you in public. You need to ask God to help you." Boy, was she right.

Two days after this incident, I was substitute teaching across the hall. During my free study period, the science teacher came over and handed me about sixty letters from students in those two unruly classes. In the letters the students apologized for their poor behavior, and they were the most sensitive letters I'd ever read—it seemed those kids had been born again. Each one asked my forgiveness, and several begged me to come back as their substitute teacher. I wept, and my tears fell onto the letters.

> Stop being angry!
>   Turn from your rage!
> Do not lose your temper—
>   it only leads to harm.
> For the wicked will be destroyed,
>   but those who trust in the LORD
>   will possess the land.
>
> PSALM 37:8–9, NLT

"I apologize for misbehaving in class—I shouldn't have been disrespectful to you," one boy's letter read. "I don't know what came over me. I know better because I was raised to obey elders. I showed very poor judgment in the classroom, and I'm really, really sorry. I truly apologize and ask that you forgive me."

While reading the letters, I could hear God saying, *Floyd, what are you going to do now?*

After asking their teacher if I could talk to each of these groups, I walked into the fourth-period class of eighth graders, carrying their letters with me. "Thank you for writing these letters," I told the students. "They have touched me deeply and I accept your apologies, but I ask your forgiveness for the way I acted. As a Christian, I shouldn't have gotten angry and yelled at you. I'm ashamed. Jesus said if we don't forgive others, He can't forgive us, and I don't want to go one day without Jesus forgiving me."

As the class fell completely silent, I choked up and left the room. The following period, I went in and said the same thing to the seventh-grade class. When I took the letters home and my wife and I read them together, I wept again.

Now, when I pass any of those students in the hallway, they smile at me and say a friendly hello. I smile back. It's like a miracle turnaround in attitude—in them and in me. When I told the school principal about the incident, he said he'd never had anything like that happen at his school before. Had I been under a teacher's contract, I couldn't have mentioned the name of Jesus, but as a substitute I'd signed no such agreement. Since that day, I haven't lost my temper in a classroom again, and the Lord is helping me keep my emotions under control in other situations as well.

Victimization and Loss

Floyd's angry response to his students was triggered by the feeling that he had lost control of the classes and that the students were not showing the proper respect for a teacher. Anger is our natural human response when we feel our perceived personal rights or expectations are violated. This may include the right to privacy, personal respect, safety, a peaceful life, having our possessions inviolate or holding and expressing an opinion.

Anger almost always begins with a perceived or actual loss of these rights, or even the threat of such a loss. Here are some of the losses we suffer that, coupled with the feeling that we have been victimized, may provoke resentment:

• Loss of control—such as being required to abide by rules we do not agree with that hamper freedoms we believe are personal rights

• Loss of effectiveness—being unable to influence the behavior of our children or other family members or friends to the extent we desire

• Loss of valued relationships—through death, infidelity, divorce, misunderstanding, hurt feelings or relocation

• Loss of a valued role—through retirement, layoff, dismissal or reassignment

• Loss of valued possessions—through carelessness, theft, floods, fires, storms or repossession of property

• Loss of skills or abilities—through accidents, injuries, debilitating illnesses or senility

• Loss of self-esteem—feeling that we have not lived up to our own standards or the standards of others

• Loss of face—through public exposure of one's failures or inadequacies, humiliation or false accusations of wrongdoing

• Loss of virginity—through illicit sex, rape or abuse

• Loss of childhood—through abandonment, separation, lack of nurturing, abuse or poverty

• Loss of protection—through threats or acts of physical harm, violence or natural disasters

Examining Our Expectations

In any relationship, we tend to bear in mind certain expectations of the other person, and of course he or she also has expectations. We seldom articulate what they are to each other—some expectations are conscious, and many are subconscious. But when one person's unspoken "list" contrasts sharply with the other's, conflict easily arises.

If pressed to put into words exactly what we expect from a relationship, we may realize with some embarrassment that our goals seem selfish or childish. And the more expectations or rights we lay claim to in a relationship, the more numerous will be our opportunities to become disappointed or angry. I (Quin) had a friend who would burst into a rage whenever her husband criticized her—which was plenty often.

"I was a Christian and had asked the Holy Spirit to guide my life—but in the area of anger, I didn't yield to His control," Josie told me. "I could not stand for a man to demean me. At the slightest hint of a put-down, I would explode with vile, hateful words. Then I would pray, 'God, somewhere in me I'm still agreeing with this anger and I'm still justifying it. I must get some satisfaction in it, or it wouldn't rise up. Lord, I don't hate this sin like You hate it. Please help me to hate it as You do.'"

> A gentle answer deflects anger, but harsh words make tempers flare. . . . A hot-tempered person starts fights; a cool-tempered person stops them.
>
> PROVERBS 15:1, 18, NLT

One day during her prayer time, Josie realized God wanted her free of her rage even more than she wanted her freedom, but she had to cooperate with Him. "Lord, I commit my mouth to be used by the Holy Spirit, and I will not allow the enemy to use me," she prayed. "I am confessing that in Christ, I have 'a quiet and gentle spirit' and 'soft answers that turn away wrath.'"

Josie memorized Scripture verses she could declare about anger and wrath, the tongue and the condition of the heart. She asked God to forgive her for not valuing her husband

48

and for judging men, including her father. Hers was not an overnight victory. But when she finally could say calmly to her husband, "Oh, lighten up, Hon," instead of "Shut up, you jerk," she realized the Holy Spirit was helping her win the battle over anger. She was learning to allow the Holy Spirit to tame her tongue.

Anger Based on False Impressions

It is shocking to see how false impressions can sometimes cause a person to resent another individual, when there is really no basis for it. Sherry saw this sticky situation develop in her own family, yet she felt helpless to resolve the issue. She shares her story:

I watched from the sidelines as the war between my husband and my mother only seemed to intensify as years went by. It was so bad that I began asking people for prayer before holiday events or birthday gatherings. Often, it would get so miserable to be around them that I wished we had skipped the party! Prayer did help, but the results were temporary. Then I got aggressive in prayer and fasting for a genuine breakthrough in my family for this issue and other things.

By now my mother had moved out of state, and I felt relieved that the stress in my life lessened. When she called one day to say she'd had a dream about me, I said, "Tell me about it." She told me her dream went something like this:

I came to see you, and you were in an old, blue house robe. The children were small. I didn't think you were being taken care of by your husband, so when he came through the door, I said to him, "Hello, 'Fred'—I haven't seen you in so long that I forgot your name!" [His name is Mike.] He got angry and went out, slamming the door behind him.

Then the scene changed, and I saw a man walking down to the beach. By the way he was walking and looking down, I figured he planned to drown himself in the ocean. Then a few minutes later, he came back brushing his hands together as if he'd let go of his burdens in the sea, and he said, "That takes care of that!"

The Lord sometimes helps me interpret dreams, so I told Mom I'd get back to her after I had time to think and pray about hers. Later that day, I called her back with an explanation.

"Mom, you've wondered what went wrong in your relationship with Mike," I told her. "The first scene in the dream shows that you felt he wasn't taking good care of me years ago when the children were small, so you became offended. It was you who started the animosity between the two of you.

"The second scene in your dream conveyed a message that 'things aren't always as they appear,'" I told her. "You thought the man was going to drown himself, but instead he was throwing his troubles into the sea. In my life and marriage, it also wasn't as it appeared to you. Mike has taken good care of me.

"Mama, let me pray with you," I finished. As I prayed, I saw it was because my mother loved me that she took up an offense on my behalf. Then I began to cry, because in my heart I'd never felt that she truly loved me. So here we were on the phone, miles apart—me getting healed of my doubt in her love and my mother getting set free of her anger and animosity toward my husband.

When Mama came for Christmas that year, it was absolutely amazing. God has healed the relationship between her and Mike, and the rest of the family noticed. One of the kids even tried to stir something up by saying, "You two haven't gotten into anything yet."

"We're doing just fine, thank you," Mama replied.

Learning Not to Judge

If we do not deal with our negative emotions head-on, they soon can control our behavior. Joan learned this painful lesson through the turbulent relationship she had with her twenty-year-old son, Don, who lived with her in an apartment in England.

He would promise her he would do something, but when he did not follow through, she continually nagged him. He would ask her to buy a gift he could give his girlfriend and promise to repay her, for example, but repayment was never forthcoming. He was always asking favors but not living up to his word.

> Everyone should be quick to listen, slow to speak and slow to become angry, for man's anger does not bring about the righteous life that God desires.
>
> JAMES 1:19–20, NIV

For Joan, the boiling point came when he was getting ready to move out of their apartment for a transfer to Holland. "Pack up all your stuff and take it with you—my lease is running out, and I can't handle all your things," she told him one day.

"I will tomorrow, I promise," he replied. But he did not. Time was running out.

Late one night, she awoke from a sound sleep. As thoughts of Don's selfish behavior swirled through her mind, she realized how angry she was with him. How could he treat her like this when she had done so much for him? She got up and went into his room, only to discover he had not started packing—had not even come home that night. The deadline for his trip was near.

Joan's uncle, the only other Christian in her family, had given her some money to pass on to Don for his trip. In her mind, Don did not deserve the money. Suddenly she felt the Lord ask her, *Have I ever helped you? Have I done things for you that you didn't deserve?*

"Yes, Lord," she answered. "You've done many things for me that I didn't deserve. Oh, Lord, please forgive me for judging," she prayed.

"I got down on the floor on my face, I was so humbled," Joan recalled. "All the stored-up anger left me as I repented before the Lord. I realized my uncle had given that money in love for my son, without conditions. Yet because Don had so hurt and disappointed me, I wanted to put conditions on it. The next morning I gave him the money and told him how I felt. Because God had reminded me of His unconditional love that I could never deserve, I was able to release the money to Don without resentment. Through this experience, I've learned a new depth of forgiveness."

When we choose to stop judging people, God will release His healing and wholeness to us. Does that mean we will not be disappointed again by the very person who originally hurt us? Not necessarily. Today, Joan is raising Don's fifteen-year-old daughter, whom she has adopted.

Are You Stuck in Traffic?

Recently I (Ruthanne) heard a conference speaker pose this thought-provoking question: Are you at a place in your life where you feel you are "stuck in traffic" on the way to something important? Or could it be that God has positioned you in that place for His higher purpose?

At the conference, Gail McWilliams shared an amazing testimony of how God gave her and her husband, Tony, five miracle children. However, during the second pregnancy doctors told her that unless she aborted the child, she would lose her eyesight. Against the doctor's advice, she chose her child over her vision and went on to have three more children. Today she inspires audiences everywhere with her message of life.

I also listened to Gail share how she and Tony encountered an impossible traffic jam one morning in Dallas on their way to a studio where they were to be interviewed on live television. Rather annoyed that Tony had not planned to leave earlier, Gail called the producer to let him know they would not make it in time. "No problem," he told her. "We can cover today's show and reschedule you later."

> But now you yourselves are to put off all these: anger, wrath, malice, blasphemy, filthy language out of your mouth. . . . Put on tender mercies, kindness, humility, meekness, longsuffering; bearing with one another, and forgiving one another.
>
> COLOSSIANS 3:8, 12–13

Just then, the car in front of them stopped suddenly. The woman driver got out, opened the back door, took a small child from the car seat and began screaming for help—her baby was having a seizure. Tony ran to her aid, called 9-1-1 for help and followed the operator's instructions to keep the child breathing. Soon a health professional stopped to help, and within minutes the child was airlifted to a hospital for treatment. Gail firmly believes that God positioned them in that situation on that particular day for a purpose greater than their getting to the TV interview.[2]

Instead of becoming upset when unexpected interruptions and delays spoil our well-laid plans, we can ask God to use us even in the midst of our frustrations. Elisabeth Elliot reminds us that difficulties and conflict actually can help mold our character:

A spirit of calm contentment always accompanies true godliness. The deep peace that comes from deep trust in God's lovingkindness is not destroyed even by the worst of circumstances, for those Everlasting Arms are still cradling us, we are always "under the Mercy." Corrie ten Boom was "born to trouble" like the rest of us, but in a German concentration camp she jumped to her feet every morning and exuberantly sang "Stand Up, Stand Up for Jesus!"

. . . Everything about which we are tempted to complain may be the very instrument whereby the Potter intends to shape His clay into the image of His Son.[3]

A Caregiver's Struggle

Finding calm in the midst of stormy family circumstances is a huge challenge. Surviving a fourteen-year storm seems unimaginable, but the woman in our next story declares that yes, it is indeed possible.

When Barb's husband, Ralph, suffered a stroke at seventy-two, she had no idea how difficult her life would become. The right side of his body was paralyzed, and his brain function and speech were so impaired he could utter only a few words. Rather than leaving him in a veterans' facility in another state, Barb decided to take care of him herself at home—though the social worker advised against it. Since she was much younger than Ralph and in good health, Barb insisted she could manage once she got Ralph settled in their small mobile home. She shared the frustrating emotions that plagued her during that troublesome time:

- Anger and frustration—because she could not meet all of Ralph's demands and because so many of her needs went unmet
- Guilt—because some of her own wrong decisions meant she had little respite
- Helplessness—because she could not communicate fully with Ralph

- Embarrassment—because she had to make excuses if people wanted to visit and Ralph refused
- Offense—because almost every day, she found herself having to forgive her husband for inflicting emotional pain on her

Ralph refused to take speech therapy, choosing to grunt words or commands that Barb alone understood. Once a joyful Christian who played trumpet in big-name bands, he now was a grouchy invalid who controlled her with his tirades.

"Mama, dump urinal!" he would scream as soon as Barb would lie down to sleep, though she had just tucked him in for the night. Refusing a hospital bed, he preferred a recliner in the living room. He never wanted Barb to leave him and wanted absolutely no visitors, though a few people from their church would stop by for short talks.

The protein shakes Barb prepared were his main sustenance since he could barely feed himself. She would also lift him, bathe him and tend to his personal hygiene needs, providing such good care that he never got a bedsore. On Sundays when she would slip off to early church while he was still asleep, she often came home to find him sitting in a messy chair, which she believed he soiled on purpose. How she dreaded the arduous cleaning, washing and disinfecting this required of her.

Occasionally, when Barb found herself impatiently slamming doors, she would ask, "Why me, Lord? What did I do to deserve this?" Then she would repent, "Oh, Lord, I'm sorry. Help me serve my husband as I would serve Christ. Help me keep calm."

Every morning Barb knelt and prayed aloud near Ralph's chair, hoping he would realize that she was calling on God to help them through another day. The only way she could remain calm despite such turmoil was through prayer and daily Bible reading, enjoying a thirty-minute bike ride during his afternoon nap, going to church on Sundays and taking Communion, and calling friends to pray with her when Ralph was out of earshot.

Barb's routine was to get up at 2:30 A.M. for her time with the Lord. She would lie on the floor and praise God, then sit in a chair to read her Bible and devotional book. She would record what God was saying to her, then nap until daylight, when yet another day of caregiving began. Year after year Ralph's condition worsened, until Barb was unable to lift him. To bathe him, she would haul pans of hot water out on the deck and give him a sponge bath and shampoo while he sat in his wheelchair.

> Better to be patient than powerful; better to have self-control than to conquer a city.
>
> PROVERBS 16:32, NLT

Though he was not in pain, Ralph's demands grew worse as the years went by. Many times Barb feared they would not make it financially, but God always provided. When worries assaulted her mind, she would begin praising God aloud for His many provisions and blessings, and through that her calm was restored. One Scripture reassured her: "You will keep him in perfect peace, whose mind is stayed on You, because he trusts in You" (Isaiah 26:3). Not until eight days before Ralph's death at home from an abdominal aneurysm did hospice step in to help her.

Statistics cannot give the full picture, but one estimate is that some 39 million households deal with the dilemma Barb faced, with about 75 percent of caregivers being women. A common problem is caregiver stress, in which the emotional strain takes a toll on a caregiver's physical and emotional health. Some suffer from depression. Many put their own needs aside, as Barb did, while devoting endless time and effort to their caregiving tasks.[4]

Looking back on her own experience, Barb offers caregivers these suggestions for staying calm and taking good care of themselves so they can take care of others:

- Establish a daily routine. It makes it easier for both you and your patient.

- Do not lose contact with the Body of Christ—you need Christian friends who will visit you, phone you and bring a meal now and then. Have friends pray with you consistently.

- Take time for yourself, and hire someone to help. Not doing this was my big regret.

- Try to get as much sleep and rest as you can. When your patient naps, lie down yourself.

- Make an effort to exercise every day. For me it was biking.

- Try to stay positive and find something to laugh about. Remember happier times you can reminisce about, talking to the patient as though he or she understands you.

- Take one day at a time, asking God for wisdom, direction and discernment for that day.

- Keep healthy by eating right. Schedule regular physical checkups for yourself.

- Guard against taking an offense. Live in a state of forgiveness and gratefulness. Do not expect to be appreciated, but know that God takes notice of your service.

As most of us know firsthand, staying calm under pressure is difficult without the Holy Spirit's help. Let's invite Him to help us keep our composure and see His higher purpose when situations and circumstances push us to react wrongly. In the next chapter, we will continue to discuss how we can overcome some other difficult challenges, particularly those that bring on worry, fear or grief.

Prayer

Lord, I know it's not Your desire that I let my emotions get out of hand and cause me to sin. Even in the midst of life's storms, help me stay calm and overcome in those areas where I'm weakest. May Your Holy Spirit walk with me, teach me and help me develop the fruit of the Spirit, I ask in Jesus' name, Amen.

4

Lord, Take Away My Worry, Fear and Grief

For you did not receive a spirit that makes you a slave again to fear, but you received the Spirit of sonship. And by him we cry, "Abba, Father." The Spirit himself testifies with our spirit that we are God's children.

Romans 8:15–16, NIV

Our lives are full of supposes. Suppose this should happen, or suppose that should happen; what could we do; how could we bear it? But, if we are living in the "high tower" of the dwelling place of God, all these supposes will drop out of our lives. . . . Even when walking through the valley of death, the psalmist could say, "I will fear no evil;" and if we are dwelling in God, we can say so too.

—Hannah Whitall Smith[1]

Worry, fear and grief are universal problems in today's world— yes, even among Christians. Throughout the Bible, we read

God's promises assuring us that we can overcome, but walking out those promises is no easy matter. Many of us still suffer from fear of rejection or abandonment, fear of failure, fear of financial lack, fear of the future, fear of illness, fear of death or fear of losing a relationship or a loved one.

In one sense, fear can be a good thing when it motivates us to take safety precautions—such as when a weather alert interrupts a broadcast or a tornado siren goes off, warning people to seek safe shelter. But irrational anxiety and fear can lead to oppression, which not only hinders our Christian growth, but negatively influences our children and those close to us.

Faith and trust in God's Word are the antidote to fear, enabling the believer to step into a new realm of trust and hope. This comes when we acknowledge our fears, repent for our lack of trust in Him, develop a strong foundation in Scripture and receive the liberty the Holy Spirit can give. Then we are really living free!

Worry—A Companion to Fear

Corrie ten Boom once said, "Worry is a cycle of inefficient thoughts whirling around a center of fear."[2]

If you do not think you have this problem, ask yourself when the last time was that you worried. Worry sends a signal that we have not placed our trust in God. In fact, obsessive worry is an expression of unbelief. Jesus' instruction to us is clear:

> Therefore I say to you, do not worry about your life, what you will eat or what you will drink; nor about your body, what you will put on. . . . Do not worry about tomorrow, for tomorrow will worry about its own things. Sufficient for the day is its own trouble.
>
> Matthew 6:25, 34

One Bible commentator writes, "Worry means 'to divide into parts.' The word suggests a distraction, a preoccupation with things causing anxiety, stress and pressure. Jesus speaks against worry and anxiety because of the watchful care of a heavenly Father who is ever mindful of our daily needs."[3]

I (Quin) once read an article called "Wait to Worry" by Fred Smith. It described a survey of four thousand worriers and revealed that:

- 40 percent of what people worry about has already happened, so they can do nothing about it.
- Another 30 percent of what they worry about could never happen.
- 22 percent of what they worry about, if it comes, will have so little effect that it isn't worth worrying about.
- By process of elimination, only 8 percent of our worries are "worth the worry."[4]

I read this at a time when I was worried about a single daughter whose city apartment had been entered and robbed. By the time I finished reading the article and all the Scriptures Smith quoted, I was ready to trade my worry for trust in God for my daughter's protection.

Many of us probably need to purposefully resist worry, anxiety and fear and step into a new realm of trust and hope. Consider these verses: "Commit your works to the LORD, and your thoughts will be established" (Proverbs 16:3) and "Be anxious for nothing, but in everything by prayer and supplication, with thanksgiving, let your requests be made known to God; and the peace of God . . . will guard your hearts and minds through Christ Jesus" (Philippians 4:6–7).

Disappointment Leads to Fear

Sometimes the pain of a failed relationship causes a person to fear ever becoming vulnerable and trusting someone again. Inevitably, this also affects a person's relationship with God. Bob Ross once was close to the Lord, but after his troubled marriage ended in divorce, he drifted away. Though he changed jobs and relocated, he failed to address the spiritual root of his problems. Random dating and several inappropriate relationships left him empty and frustrated. Bob shares his experience in his own words:

One evening I was feeling especially despondent and unhappy with my life. I was hungry for a relationship, but the ones I'd had up until then had been less than satisfying. I hadn't prayed for a long time, but on this day I knelt beside my bed and told Abba Father how lonely I was.

I ended my prayer by asking God for a relationship with a Christian lady. "But I'm not asking for another wife, as I'm not sure I'm ready for that again," I told the Lord. "I've already had too much pain, and I don't need any more."

The next day when I asked my landlady to recommend a church, she suggested I ask the three "church ladies" who lived across the street. I did, and they invited me to attend a service with them that Sunday. This was the beginning of my returning to the Lord. The congregation He led me to was an answer to a prayer I hadn't even prayed.

Once in church again, I forgot about my bedside prayer—but God didn't. I developed a friendship with each of these ladies, and over time, I became more than friends with one, Janice. As our relationship grew more serious, I grew anxious—my divorce was still an open wound causing me much pain. Certain that I couldn't handle another such experience, I was afraid of the possibility of marriage. My fear was growing faster than my relationship with Janice.

One evening, while driving down a quiet road and crying out to God about this, I poured out all my fear and pain. After I quieted down, God reminded me of my prayer for

> The Lord is my light and my
> salvation;
> Whom shall I fear?
> The Lord is the strength of my life;
> Of whom shall I be afraid?
>
> Psalm 27:1

a "Christian lady." Then He asked me a simple question: *If you can't trust Me, who can you trust?*

At that point my fears evaporated. I knew I could trust my Abba. A short time later I asked Janice to be my wife, and God has blessed us mightily over these twenty-plus years we have been married. He answered my prayer and took away my fear, and my life has never been the same.

Ruled by Fear

Bob's story shows us how fear can engulf adults and affect their ability to form meaningful relationships. But beyond adult concerns, many adults still deal with fears they experienced in their youth. Those fears, born out of experiences they had while young, may impact their lives for years to come. That was the case for LeeAnn, now a married mother of three.

As an insecure fifteen-year-old with hardly any friends, she had been thrilled when Tony, a popular senior, suddenly took an interest in her. But before long, he turned jealous and controlling, dictating what she wore and whom she spent time with. Then he became physically, sexually and emotionally abusive.

"I was scared of Tony," LeeAnn said, "but he controlled me by telling me that if I left him, he would tell my parents we were having sex. His tactics kept me isolated and full of fear for almost a year. When my parents did find out the truth, I was brokenhearted by their disappointment in me and their shame at my behavior. Yet I was afraid to tell them about Tony's abuse, and I had no one else to talk to."

Though LeeAnn was too entrenched in Tony's control to walk away from him, her parents forced the relationship to stop. Her mom took her for a pregnancy test, which thankfully was negative, but the stress and upheaval LeeAnn endured left her emotionally traumatized.

"I thought if I could shove all this pain in a box and blame it on something specific, I could handle it better," she said. "I had gained weight, so I stuffed all my hurts into a box called 'fear of getting fat.' I felt that gave me more control of my life. After losing weight, I was happy again—or so I thought."

By the time she was sixteen, LeeAnn had connected with new friends and felt life was good. Yet a nagging sense of worthlessness distressed her as she swung between being on top of the world one day and in the depths of despair the next, plagued by suicidal thoughts. She began writing dark poems.

"I had told no one about the abuse, and my box called 'fear of getting fat' was getting bigger," she said. "By now I had developed an eating disorder and truly feared that if I gained weight, my world would collapse." LeeAnn was a serious student of ballet, and for a dancer, being thin was paramount to being successful. But thinness did not keep her depression and suicidal feelings from increasing, and she struggled to keep her brokenness hidden from others.

"After I turned seventeen, I was on the way to a friend's house one day when the 'infection bubble' inside of me burst," she reported. "I cried and cried as buried memories and pain poured into my mind and broken heart. When I got to my friend's house, I told her about the abuse I had suffered, knowing I could trust her. Without judging, she just listened to me and comforted me."

Sharing her pain caused the cloud of darkness to begin lifting and started LeeAnn on the road to recovery. Although she was still dealing with the eating disorder when she began college, God guarded her from further destruction. In her second year, a series of frightening dreams sent her searching the Bible for verses on protection. After reading Scriptures at night, she would pray that she could sleep without being chased by demons in her dreams.

> In the multitude of my anxieties within me,
> Your comforts delight my soul.
> PSALM 94:19

"Soon I had an awareness of God—that He was silently there with me," she said. "The demonic dreams stopped, and I began writing poems about God. After becoming engaged, I rewrote the words to hymns to use for my wedding. About a year after getting married, I was truly born again and filled with the Holy Spirit. Then the Lord slowly began pulling up the weeds of unforgiveness from my heart and dealing with my fears and soul-wound issues.

"I forgave Tony for abusing me, realizing that he had been hurt by a cruel father. When I saw him in a store not long ago, I knew my forgiveness was real, because I felt no pain or fear. Through more prayer ministry and counseling, I was set free from my eating disorder and the fear of getting fat. I recognized that my need to control—my way of dealing with things I had no power over—was sinful and not the way to fix a problem. God has healed my broken heart and completely set me free."

Like LeeAnn, many of us face situations where we can deliberately choose to close the door on the pain of our past once and for all and move on with God's plan for our lives.

But that is not to say we will not have new challenges to face along the way.

Fear of the Future

When life seems to be going well, we have little cause to be afraid, but when a crisis hits, we discover the true strength of our faith. A cold fear gripped Marie when her doctor told her she had Parkinson's disease, a central nervous system disorder that impairs motor skills and speech. She started dragging her right leg during her daily walks, then developed tremors in her right hand and often felt so weak she could no longer clean house or work in the yard. Probably worse than the debilitating symptoms was the fear that haunted her.

"I was devastated by the diagnosis," Marie said. "Besides having bouts of weakness, my feet began to curl in like claws, my leg muscles cramped and it seemed my legs were shutting down. *Why do I have this?* I wondered, as no similar disease existed in my family background. Fearful of the future, I became so discouraged, I asked the Lord to take me home."

> For God has not given us a spirit of fear, but of power and of love and of a sound mind.
>
> 2 TIMOTHY 1:7

Then one day God sent a friend to Marie's house to pray for her. They started meeting every week, praying Scripture prayers right out of the Bible and focusing on her health and their families.

"Our faith would build and sometimes soar as we'd claim healing verses," Marie said. "Twice I dreamed that I was walking normally without my leg dragging. How I prayed that dream would come to pass! God showed me that I had opened a door to fear—especially fear of the future—plus rejection, abandonment and hopelessness. Whenever a negative memory surfaced, I'd repent, pray for healing in that area and ask the Holy Spirit to renew my mind and heart."

For more than six years, Marie stood on the promises of Scripture and meditated on verses about hope. "I knew the same Spirit that raised Christ from the dead was living in me," she said. "I would declare aloud, 'God is my hope—no person or doctor is my hope. Because of Jesus' shed blood, I have hope.'"

Seven years after her diagnosis, Marie began walking without a limp, then was able to work in her yard without difficulty. In fact, it seemed she now had supernatural strength—enough to use the riding lawn mower around her house while singing praise choruses.

"Healing is a process, and I continue to do battle using God's Word as my weapon," Marie said. "My hopelessness has been replaced with new faith and trust in God's promises as I live every day to please and praise Him. And I have no fear of the future!"

What Is the Root of Fear?

Can our grandparents' habits or behavior have any sway over us? Maybe you have not considered the possibility that a pattern of sin in your ancestry can have any effect on your life today. As Christians, we must acknowledge that many of the problems we experience are due to our own disobedience to God and His Word. Yet some of our struggles and patterns of behavior might stem from our familial lines.

We see certain sin patterns or habits in biblical families. Abraham, for example, lied about his wife, Sarah, calling her his sister on two occasions. Later Abraham's son Isaac lied about his wife, Rebekah, saying she was his sister. Isaac's son Jacob deceived his father in order to receive the firstborn blessing due his older brother, Esau. Then Jacob's sons deceived him about his son Joseph, causing him to believe the young man was dead.

The tendency to lie and deceive showed up in succeeding generations, each time causing more serious consequences. The blessings of Abraham far outweighed the innate tendency toward sin, but Scripture reveals that the sins of the fathers did have a powerful negative impact on their progeny.

So yes, we may tend to be "bent or crooked" in our susceptibility to sin in the same areas that troubled our forefathers. The enemy knows where our weak areas are because he has been working against our ancestors for generations.

Author Catherine Marshall called this "the law of generational weakness" when she realized some fears that controlled her were rooted in experiences with her Grandmother Sarah, who had taken care of her for several months when she was young. In her book *Something More*, she writes:

> So strong is the Law of Generations that even what we scorn can still come down to us. In my case it was not Grandmother Sarah's particular fears—rather simply an over-inclination to fear. In my life it centered on a dread of germs and illnesses, a horror of mice and small dead animals, and during my childhood, fear of the dark, ghosts, and the like. The time came when I realized that in Jesus' eyes, fear is a sin since it is acting out a lack of trust in God.[5]

What did she do about it? She studied the Bible and came to some conclusions:

> It soon became apparent that just as we can inherit either a fortune or debts, so in the spiritual realm we can inherit either spiritual blessings or those liabilities (unabashedly called "sins" in Scripture) that hinder our development into mature persons.[6]

With a desire to break her tendency to allow fear to overwhelm her, she asked her son, Peter, to join her in prayer. His prayer went something like this:

Lord Jesus, You came to earth to . . . set every captive free. Lord, Mother has been captive to these fears that we're laying out before You. Yet You've declared that where the Spirit of the Lord is, there is liberty. So now, Lord, I take that Word . . . and wielding it as the Sword of the Spirit that it is, in Your Name and by Your power, I hereby cut Mother free from every chain and shackle from the past. I release her now to her rightful heritage.

Catherine's final step was to praise God. "We found that the release would not be final unless I received it in faith, and as I had been discovering, praise is the swiftest, surest route to faith," she wrote, adding that she was actually set free from fear.[7]

Fear can come through many avenues, often from our past. If you are plagued by intense fear, ask the Lord to show you its source. Perhaps you were hurt in some sort of accident or on a school playground, or were mistreated by a trusted adult. Maybe fear began to grip you in a hospital surgical ward where you almost died, or when you experienced a frightening storm or witnessed a traumatic event. If you lost a parent through death or divorce during childhood, you may struggle with a fear of abandonment. If you have lost your husband to another woman, fear of trusting men may be a stronghold.

Whatever the source of your fear, you can find freedom through faith in the Word of God. You have the option to choose faith over fear.

Healing Grief

A common cause of fear and worry is the onslaught of grief—that heart-stabbing emotion that all of us eventually experience in life. Whether it stems from the death of a loved one, a divorce, a broken friendship, a lost job or some other disappointment, grief is a part of our sinful heritage that is certain to come. The question is, how will we respond to it?

Expressing grief in appropriate ways provides an escape channel for our painful emotions, as a tea kettle's valve allows steam to discharge. This helps us acknowledge the loss, resolve the pain, then move forward in trusting God with the future. Do not let the rest of your life be defined by a loss you have suffered. It is important not to get "stuck" in the grief through denial, depression or blaming. Even in the midst of grief, we have hope because we have access to the promises of God and His comfort.

Let's examine how one woman made her way through the grieving process:

Renee and Scott had been married just one year when he was diagnosed with colon cancer. Over the next three years, he bravely tried every way he could to overcome it. Two other men in their church had survived cancer, and Renee strongly believed that Scott would be healed. But after almost two months in the hospital, he died, and Renee's world suddenly came crashing down. "God, where are You?" she cried in her grief.

"I went into a dark pit and felt like I was dying," she told me (Quin). "I was so disappointed in God, feeling He had let me down. At night I'd curl up in bed and cry my eyes out, but I only shared my sorrow with a few close friends. Although I went through the functions of life, all I felt for a full year was grief and emptiness."

Two concerned friends suggested that if Renee would go to the Brownsville revival in Florida, they would pray and fast for her to come out of her darkness. She agreed to go if one of them would accompany her. After they entered the building and found seats, Renee prayed silently, *Lord, if You don't heal my heart right now, tonight, I might never get healed.*

As the congregation began spontaneously worshiping—the most beautiful sound Renee had ever heard—someone passed her a note that read: "You will know whether this is from the Lord, but as I was standing in line, I believe the Lord gave me this word for you. He says, 'I see your heart and I will heal your heart this night.'" What amazing confirmation!

> Yea, though I walk through the valley of the shadow of death, I will fear no evil;
> For You are with me;
> Your rod and Your staff, they comfort me.
>
> PSALM 23:4

"The congregation continued singing, and I felt the Lord's hand on my chest, warm and loving," Renee said. "He was touching me, caressing my heart. I felt such inner happiness, a smile spread across my face. In fact, I couldn't stop smiling."

The next evening she returned for another service and met the man who had passed the note to her. Encouraged by her testimony, he could see the evidence in her countenance. Renee returned home to Tennessee, got more involved in her church and joined the dance team.

"I put on my garment of praise and danced before the Lord with such joy," she said. "I even started a ministry for hurting people called the Melting Pot, and within a short time we had prayed for more than a hundred people. I went on my first missions trip, then another—four in all. On one trip, I met my future husband. God has healed my broken heart and restored joy and purpose to my life."

Recovery Is a Process

The journey out of grief will not be the same for everyone because different personalities respond in different ways.

Some take longer than others to go through this valley that is unique for each person. After I (Ruthanne) unexpectedly lost my husband, John, through a sudden heart attack more than five years ago, it seemed I wandered in a fog of unreality for several months.

When I actually began experiencing the stages of grief, I discovered they require enormous spiritual, emotional and physical energy. I sometimes felt guilty because a relatively small task took longer than I thought it should to complete, leaving me exhausted but often unable to sleep. My prayer partner helped me understand that grieving is like work. I needed to acknowledge that fact and make allowances for fatigue by limiting my commitments.

My solution for sleeplessness was—and still is today—to meditate on God's many blessings in my life while playing soft instrumental worship music. It helps me focus on the Lord instead of on any problems I may have so that I can relax and sleep.

Some people become so overwhelmed by the effort involved in recovering from loss that they seek to avoid the process. But avoidance does not substitute for grieving—it only postpones it. Consider the four major tasks of grief:

- Acceptance, or simply facing the reality that you have suffered the loss. The greater the loss, the more difficult this task will be.
- Experiencing the pain. Our aversion to pain causes us to want to avoid this step. Some people medicate their anguish with alcohol or drugs, or numb it through work, socializing, busyness, travel or other means. But the pain needs to be acknowledged and felt so that healing can come—and for most, tears are a part of the healing.

- Adjusting to an environment where the deceased (or the lost relationship, job or goal) is not present. This means the mourner must believe in himself or herself, learn new skills and take on new responsibilities. Those who already lack self-confidence or have few job skills find this difficult, but the joy of the Lord truly can become their strength to move forward.

- Reorganizing activities by taking steps to return to a more balanced, normal life. Some find it easier to hold on to memories of the past rather than taking the risks involved in reinvesting in the future. Certainly this final phase is not easy, but God's grace and wisdom to aid in the process are only a prayer away.

Laughing Helps Grief

Barbara Johnson, the late author and humorist, has helped many people on their journey of grief by getting them to laugh. Despite multiple tragedies in her own life, Barbara was one of the most joyful people we have ever met—not because she ignored the calamities in her life, but because she learned to laugh in spite of them. She wrote:

> Humor helps to combat my own grief and helps me accelerate the grief process for others. I love little quips and quotes and have collected hundreds of them over the years. Humor is not something to be used to make fun of a situation, only to make fun out of what seems to be a hopeless catastrophe. Folks need something that will help get them through the times when nothing seems to calm them, not even reminders of comfort from the Bible given by well-meaning Christian friends. It's not that these scriptures aren't true; it's just that the pain is so intense you can't appreciate what the words are saying right at that moment.

Later these scripture verses can become very meaningful, but, ironically, there were times during my own sieges of grief that the following observation made a kind of crazy sense to me: "Man cannot live by bread alone; he needs peanut butter, too."[8]

> God is our merciful Father and the source of all comfort. He comforts us in all our troubles so that we can comfort others. When they are troubled, we will be able to give them the same comfort God has given us.
>
> 2 CORINTHIANS 1:3–4, NLT

Barbara helps us not to take ourselves too seriously and to indulge in laughter from time to time to avoid falling into despair. Though well acquainted with grief—out of her four sons, one died in Vietnam and another in a car accident, and a third was estranged from her for many years—Barbara knew how much laughing helps in the midst of grieving.

Another woman's experience illustrates that reaching out to someone else can lighten our own burden of grief. Ruth Sissom, a widow, shared how she decided to visit a woman in her church who was grief-stricken over the loss of her husband.

"Offering myself in an effort to assist the healing of others had a restorative effect on me," Ruth wrote later. "It was the most effective way I found to promote healing for my own lonely heart."[9]

Disappointment and loss are never pleasant. But when they come, as they will, they can provide seasons of spiritual growth in which we draw closer to the God who loves us.

In our next chapter, we will confront another topic that also provides us an opportunity for spiritual growth. It is one of the biggest traps the enemy uses against us, and one that most of us have fallen prey to many times over—unforgiveness.

PRAYER

Heavenly Father, help me cast my worries, fears and sorrows upon You and receive Your comfort. Thank You in advance for delivering me from fretting over things I can't change. Lord, as You begin the healing process in my heart, help me trust You completely for strength to face the future. Thank You for Your promise that You will never forsake me. Amen.

5

Lord, Enable Me to Forgive

If you forgive men their trespasses, your heavenly Father will also forgive you. But if you do not forgive men their trespasses, neither will your Father forgive your trespasses.

Matthew 6:14–15

How soon we all forget the greatness of grace which looked beyond our faults and, seeing our needs, totally forgave us. . . . Our sin seems too small in comparison; our guilt, somehow, not as failing as those who fail us. Yet amid all this Jesus calls *us* into accountability—to an accounting for our ease in forgetting the dimensions of our deliverance.

—Jack Hayford[1]

"Forgive him? You've got to be kidding."

How many times have we thought or said this when someone hurt us? Probably more times than we can count. Our tendency is to indulge our grievances and hold on to our bitterness by telling ourselves, *After all he (she) did, this person doesn't deserve to be forgiven.* The truth is, none of us deserves forgiveness.

What, exactly, does it mean to forgive? We find several shades of meaning both from dictionary and biblical definitions of the word:

- to cancel a debt or absolve from payment
- to excuse from a fault or an offense
- to renounce anger or resentment against
- to give up the wish to punish or to get even
- to bestow a favor unconditionally
- to release, unchain or set at liberty[2]

The heart of the Gospel is that Jesus, who died on the cross to cancel our huge debt of sin, willingly forgives us when we confess and repent. That is, He willingly forgives us if we choose to forgive those who trespass against us, as Matthew 6:14 instructs.

Refusing to forgive someone actually will prevent us from receiving forgiveness ourselves! But once we decide to obey Scripture and call on the Lord's help, the Holy Spirit empowers us to make our decision to forgive someone stick. Only then can our wounded emotions be healed.

"To forgive is like acquitting a defendant, clearing him even if he's guilty, and dealing with him as though innocent," explained our friend Pastor Dutch Sheets in one of his sermons. "It's like freeing him from prison, chains or bondage."

No Regrets

Becky LaRose believes it pays to walk in forgiveness because it will keep you from suffering regrets later in life. She and her husband, Paul, regularly prayed for their four children, but they focused especially on their oldest, Neil, when he became rebellious and got involved in drugs and alcohol in high school. To keep his behavior from adversely affecting his younger siblings, they had Neil move out of their home twice. When he graduated, Becky wrote a loving letter expressing her pride in his achievements and encouraging him that he could do much good for the world.

"For seven years we had prayed Neil would come to his own faith in Christ, not just inherit ours," Becky told me (Quin). "I copied parts of your book *How to Pray for Your Children* into my prayer journal to inspire me to keep praying even when I couldn't see one good thing happening in the natural. When Neil went away to college, we prayed for God to reveal Himself to our son, even to shake him and wake him in the middle of the night, but also to extend His mercy and protection."

On the evening of Thanksgiving Day during Neil's first semester, God suddenly stepped into the silence of this young man's life. While studying alone in his apartment, Neil heard the Lord speak to him. Surely it was a shaking and waking moment for the nineteen-year-old. Early the next morning, he phoned his parents with exciting news.

"Last night I heard God's voice in my bedroom!" he exclaimed. "I know what life is all about now—I know what I'm here for." Then he read them the list of "things God told me" from his notebook, along with several Scripture verses. One of his favorites was "The fear of the LORD is the beginning of wisdom, and knowledge of the Holy One is understanding" (Proverbs 9:10, NIV).

For the next couple of days, Neil preached to his friends and to strangers, sharing his experience and asking them about their beliefs in God. But on the third day after Neil's divine visitation, Becky and Paul got the phone call no parent ever wants to receive. A trauma surgeon in the city where Neil lived told them their son had been in a serious car accident and they should come immediately.

Walking into the hospital with faith and determination to take Neil home and pray him back to health, they were not prepared to see their child unconscious and hooked up to tubes, monitors and a ventilator. Neil had hit a palm tree while driving alone. When doctors declared him brain-dead, Becky and Paul agreed to the removal of all life support.

> Hope does not disappoint us, because God has poured out his love into our hearts by the Holy Spirit, whom he has given us.
> ROMANS 5:5, NIV

"We gathered the strength to go to Neil's apartment, where we found the evidence of God's visit," Becky reported. "Neil's bedroom was just as he had left it, his Bible open on his bed with the verses he had shared with us underlined in yellow marker. Later I found three letters in his school bag that I had written to him during his rebellious period, reassuring him of my love and support. It was comforting to know he took those letters with him everywhere he went.

"I've learned you must love your children unconditionally, pray persistently for God to draw them to Himself and walk in forgiveness no matter how much they break your heart. After praying for years that Neil would come to Christ and go to heaven, I know that's where he is today, waiting for us. In our last phone conversation, he told me, 'I love you, Mom.'"

Today Neil's grave marker declares the truth he discovered in answer to his parents' prayers: *The Fear of the Lord Is the Beginning of Wisdom.*

In Becky and Paul's experience, we see how painful and spiritually devastating it could have been if they had failed to forgive Neil. Instead, the benefits of forgiving their son gave them much comfort in their time of grief. In our next story, events in the lives of Sylvia and Daniel illustrate a similar lesson.

Making a Hard Choice

Upon learning that her older daughter was pregnant out of wedlock, Sylvia reacted with shock, embarrassment and anger. *Why Lori?* she asked herself. *Why us? We're church leaders, and this sort of thing is not supposed to happen!* Thinking back over Lori's childhood, she wondered where they had failed. "I questioned our parenting skills as my mask of 'having it all together' was shattered," she said.

The Lord showed her that she and Daniel were not to take the blame for Lori's decision, nor the credit for their other children who stayed on the path. Each individual is responsible for his or her own choices. Sylvia worried about her own future, though—would she be stuck at home for years to care for this child while Lori finished school and got a job? Finally, she prayed, "Lord, I am willing to do whatever it takes to help Lori parent her child."

"I saw more clearly how Jesus had taken upon Himself our pain and sin when we were helpless and hopeless," Sylvia shared. "God changed my heart, and I was able to forgive my daughter; then I truly desired to take on her pain."

After Lori and her boyfriend parted company, she gave birth to a beautiful little boy. Shortly thereafter, when distant relatives asked to adopt him, she agreed.

"I suffered the pain she felt in giving up her baby," Sylvia said, "but I knew he was going to a mother who had prayed for a child, and we could keep in contact with the family. Later, Lori recommitted her life to the Lord, finished school and married a godly young man."

Imagine Sylvia's anger and shame when her younger daughter, Marsha, got pregnant five years later. "I never expected problems from Marsha," Sylvia told us. "But late in her senior year, when a guy named Wes came on the scene, my 'sunshine girl' brought this storm into our lives. I realized anew how much Satan hates our godly offspring."

One night Marsha walked out of the house with no purse or coat after her parents had said no to her going on a date. After twenty-four hours Sylvia called the police, but because Marsha was eighteen, they said they could do nothing. When Marsha finally came home, her parents told her she had to respect and obey them or else leave. She chose to stay, but shortly afterward told them she was pregnant.

"We had a horrible time coming to terms with Marsha's deceit," Sylvia shared. "We had forbidden her to see Wes, but she wanted to marry him despite his bad reputation and our intense dislike for him. Daniel wanted to confront the young man, but instead he would get into the shower every day and cry and pray for them."

> Then Peter came to Him and said, "Lord, how often shall my brother sin against me, and I forgive him? Up to seven times?" Jesus said to him, "I do not say to you, up to seven times, but up to seventy times seven."
>
> MATTHEW 18:21–22

Sylvia and Daniel prepared a covenant for Marsha to sign. They assured her of their prayers and support as she carefully considered whether or not to marry Wes, but asked that she postpone the decision until they had peace and could give the couple their blessing. Then they listed the things they expected of her:

- She must respect curfew and tell them where she would be and when she would be home.
- She must continue working as long as possible and pay $200 a month rent.
- She must continue attending church with the family and allow members to pray for and support all of them during her pregnancy.

- After the baby's birth, she would be free to live with them or with Wes's parents, and they trusted her to make the right decision for all concerned.

"God did a work in our hearts, and we chose to forgive her," Sylvia said. "Unbeknownst to her, Daniel deposited Marsha's rent money into an account to return to her later. The ladies of the church gave her a baby shower, and she received much loving support."

After her daughter was born, Marsha chose to live with Wes's folks. The baby quickly won Sylvia's and Daniel's hearts. Seeing that Marsha and Wes truly loved one another, they gave their blessing for the marriage.

"Today both daughters are happily married, they each have two wonderful children, and they and their families are active in church," Sylvia reported. "I love both my sons-in-law and can hardly remember the pain, anger and shame of long ago. God brings us through, not around, life's difficulties. He has turned my disappointments into treasures of darkness."

No, life does not always happen the way we expected. It certainly did not for Sylvia and Daniel. But when we obey God's Word to forgive, as they did, we can trust Him to walk with us through our times of pain and despair.

Forgiveness Is a Process

For many, forgiving is a process that takes place over time. Corrie ten Boom, who forgave her Nazi captors for imprisoning her family because they hid Jews during World War II, often spoke of this. Years ago, both of us heard Corrie speak. She shared the analogy of a church sexton ringing the church bell to call people to worship.

"When he finally releases the rope, the bell continues going ding-dong-ding for a while before the sound stops," she said. "It's the same with us. If we have been pulling on the rope of unforgiveness for a long time—continually dwelling on our grievances—it may take a while before the final ding-dong of a painful memory stops. But it will stop."

I (Ruthanne) often use the following analogy to explain the forgiveness process: When you suffer an offense from someone you trust, it is like a knife stab to the heart, inflicting deep hurt. You may try to medicate the pain with alcohol, drugs, denial or seeking revenge, but before recovery can begin, you must remove the knife—just as you must do with a physical knife wound. Choosing to forgive is like pulling out the knife. The pain does not instantly disappear. But over time, though a scar may remain, the pain lessens and the wound is healed.

When we forgive by an act of our will, our emotions eventually follow suit. However, forgiving the offender does not mean that he or she gets off free. It means our thoughts and emotions are no longer in bondage to that person. We release the offender into God's hands, who is able to render judgment as only He can. The apostle Paul knew that prompting us toward unforgiveness is a strategy of the enemy to keep us from God's best. Paul wrote: "But one whom you forgive anything, I forgive also . . . so that no advantage would be taken of us by Satan, for we are not ignorant of his schemes" (2 Corinthians 2:10–11, NASB).

Our Helper, the Holy Spirit, empowers us to forgive in order to destroy the enemy's tactics, as Margarita's story demonstrates.

Forgiveness Brings Peace

When I (Ruthanne) met Margarita and heard her story, I could never have imagined the abuse and anguish this lovely young mom had endured. She opened her heart to me because she believes *breaking the silence* leads to *breaking the cycle* of abuse that holds many families captive. In her own words, Margarita relates her remarkable journey to forgiveness:

From the time I was very young, I suffered molestation from two close relatives, as well as from my father. My life was full of chaos, with an alcoholic father, a manic-depressive mother and lots of siblings in a tiny, crowded house. Many times I prayed and asked God to make my father stop his abuse, but it continued over several years.

In fifth grade, though Mom wouldn't allow me to attend sex education classes, my friends told me what they'd learned about reporting to a responsible adult if anyone touched them improperly. Then I knew for sure that what was happening to me was wrong. One day, after a terrible experience the night before, I skipped school with the hope that Mom would ask why so I could appeal to her for help. But she never asked, and I didn't know where to turn.

At age twelve, I attempted suicide by taking a handful of pills and ended up in a hospital, where the doctor called in a counselor. I only told the counselor about being abused by a relative who didn't live with us, but when he questioned my mom, she lied about it. Later she told me I had to keep quiet and not cause trouble.

Realizing there was no use reporting what Dad had done, I lost hope and became very angry at God. Though Dad didn't violate me again, the stress of feeling responsible to protect my younger siblings caused me to once more attempt suicide. When I again tried to present the facts to a counselor, Mom accused me of just trying to get attention, so I retracted my story despite my outrage.

I married at age eighteen, moved two hundred miles away and later had two daughters whom I adored. Life seemed to be going well until the school where I worked sent me to a seminar to learn to recognize signs of child abuse and how to report it. Those classes triggered a flood of dreadful memories I had managed to repress for years.

A few days later, I completely "spaced out" while on my way to class. I parked my car, got out, then wandered down the street in a daze and gave my purse to the first woman I encountered. She took me into a nearby store to get help, and they managed to reach my husband, but when he arrived I didn't even recognize him. He took me to a psychiatrist, where the truth came out in my therapy sessions.

> Judgment without mercy will be shown to anyone who has not been merciful. Mercy triumphs over judgment!
>
> JAMES 2:13, NIV

Flashbacks of the abuse I had endured made me wish to die. Slowly I regained my memory, only to sink deeper into depression after facing such a horrible reality. I stopped therapy and began drinking heavily with my husband. When he was issued three DUIs within a few months, we entered a twelve-step recovery program. About this same time, my daughters began going to a church youth group with one of their friends.

After two months in recovery, I made a trip home to confront my father for the first time. I demanded that Dad admit what he had done to me so I could see him humiliated by the shame of his actions, but he refused. He didn't deny it, however—he just wept. Then he suggested that if I had reported him back then, he might have had to go to prison to pay for what he'd done.

"You'll never be able to pay for what you did!" I screamed at him and left in fury.

After that, my family ostracized me and accused me of being cruel, which drove me to start drinking again. Then I learned my father had cancer. Recognizing that alcohol was not the answer, I went back to recovery and began journaling and writing poetry to express my deepest feelings. When my daughters began volunteering at their friend's church, I visited some of the services. Two of the ladies there reached out to me.

Before long, I got news that Dad's cancer was terminal and he had only a short time to live. At church, I discovered that God loved me even when I was sinning and mad at Him. Though I had tried on my own to change my life with no success, I realized God had given me a loving husband, beautiful daughters and some supportive friends to show me that I didn't have to walk through things alone. Now that I had found fellowship in the church, these ladies helped me make peace with God, and He changed my heart. Without sharing details, I asked them to pray that God would help me heal the relationship with my father before he died.

That week, while sorting through a box of mementos from years past, I found a photo of Dad as a little boy, a poem he had written when his mom died and other such items. For the first time I felt compassion for him, and I knew God was giving me the strength to stop hating and truly forgive him. It was a liberating moment.

Taking those mementos with me to Dad's hospital room, I shared them with him and the other family members present. Amazingly, there was no conflict among us. After everyone left, I stayed with Dad and read to him from my journal things I had written expressing my pain. Through tears he admitted that shame and guilt had tormented him for years; then he asked for my forgiveness. I was able to say from my heart, "I forgive you, Dad. And if you ask God to, He'll forgive you, too."

A great burden lifted off both of us that night. He died a few days later, but I'm certain that he made peace with God. Before I left, Dad told me where to find a book I had given him years earlier in which he had written poems. Some of his poems expressed his desire to find forgiveness, and I shared copies of these with family members at his funeral.

I've learned that no human power can restore us, but God can and will if only we yield to Him. Now I pray God will use me to reach Mom and restore our relationship. He has given me such love for her. None of us deserves His love and forgiveness, but I'm so grateful He gave it anyway.

While Margarita's story may seem an extreme case, it illustrates that God's love can enable a person to forgive the most heinous offense, thereby finding peace and healing. Over the years, I (Ruthanne) have met and prayed with many women battling with the dark secret of childhood sexual abuse. Yet when they go through the process of forgiving their offenders, they are restored over time. In some cases they are able to minister to other abuse victims whom God brings across their paths and lead them to healing.

Then the master called the servant in. "You wicked servant," he said, "I canceled all that debt of yours because you begged me to. Shouldn't you have had mercy on your fellow servant just as I had on you?" In anger his master turned him over to the jailers to be tortured, until he should pay back all he owed.

This is how my heavenly Father will treat each of you unless you forgive your brother from your heart.

MATTHEW 18:32–35, NIV

Of course, not all women who have been abused feel free to share their painful memories, nor should they be expected to. But simply experiencing God's love and acceptance through sensitive believers reaching out to them helps move them toward being able to forgive and have wholeness restored to their lives.

Another woman who had been abused by her father shared how she decided when she became a Christian that she needed to forgive him. First she memorized Scriptures on forgiveness and love. Then she prayed, "Lord, bless my father. I realize if he had had his mind trained on You, he would never have done what he did to me. I choose to forgive him. Now please bring him to a right, godly state of mind." The Lord did just that.

Charge It to Jesus

I (Quin) have a friend whose grown adopted son would shout, curse and blame her for all his misfortunes whenever he visited her. One afternoon as she was complaining to the Lord about this, God led her to read the book of Philemon.

Philemon is Paul's letter asking his friend to take back his runaway slave, Onesimus, whom the apostle had led to the Lord. He wrote, "If then you regard me a partner, accept him as you would me. But if he has wronged you in any way or owes you anything, charge that to my account" (Philemon 17–18, NASB).

The words "charge that to my account" practically jumped off the page for my friend. From then on, when her son hurt her feelings, she would say, "Lord, I charge it to You. You went to the cross for his sins, just as You did for mine. Now I thank You in advance for bringing him into Your Kingdom."

Today this young man teaches a midweek home Bible study, and his mom is his chief supporter and intercessor.

A counselor friend of mine tells her clients they first need to "own up" to their feelings of hurt and anger, then forgive the person for specific offenses in order to be completely set free. She suggests praying something such as "God, I forgive Dad for not being there when I needed him . . . for touching me improperly . . . for beating me . . . for not showing love . . . for being mean to Mom . . . for dying and abandoning me . . ." or whatever the situation may be.

In some cases, it is helpful when forgiving to make a list of everything you did not get (or did not get enough of) from your mother, father, husband or whoever wounded you. Or you may need to list all the reasons you are still angry at that person, then pray and specifically forgive him or her for each one. It is also beneficial to discuss these things with a counselor or prayer partner and have them pray with you. Sharing with someone you trust helps you vent your hurt feelings—an important step in the process. It also makes you accountable to a person who can help you see the situation more objectively.

By taking the following steps, you can be freed from the bondage of unforgiveness. When the offender is thus released from your judgment, God can work more freely in that person's life as well as yours.

1. Acknowledge the wounding you have suffered because of this person's actions, telling God exactly how you feel. Do not be afraid to admit that you are angry about your loss or pain.

2. Choose to forgive the person who has hurt you. Follow Jesus' example of refusing to retaliate (see 1 Peter 2:23).

3. Ask God to help you see this person from His point of view and to love him or her with His love (see Romans 5:5). Seek His guidance as to whether, or when, you should contact the person by some means to say, "I forgive you." Keep in mind that forgiving your offender does not mean you must continue to be vulnerable to abuse. Unless the person shows remorse, reconciliation may not be possible.

4. Ask God to forgive you for anger you may have felt toward Him because you feel He allowed the offense to happen. Then realize God does not overrule an offender's freedom to make choices, even evil choices.

5. Thank God for forgiving you, acknowledging that your sin against Him was greater than this person's offense

against you (see Romans 4:7–8). Freely receive His cleansing.

6. Recognize that this person had a great need in his or her life when he or she hurt you—wounded people wound others. Model Jesus' prayer in Luke 23:34: "Then Jesus said, 'Father, forgive them, for they do not know what they do.'"

7. Pray for this person; bless, do not curse. Your bitterness will fade when you are blessing your offender and praying that he or she will respond to God's grace and be set free (see Luke 6:28, 35).

8. Remember that forgiving your offender is conditional to you receiving God's forgiveness and not being hindered in your spiritual growth (see Matthew 6:14–15).

9. Determine that you will not dwell on the hurts of the past. When painful thoughts and feelings come, declare to the enemy, "That's forgiven and under the blood of Jesus!"

10. Finally, be careful how you talk about what happened to hurt you. As one pastor said, "Stop nursing and rehearsing your hurts." Only share your story as God leads, when you have an opportunity to help someone else struggling with a similar issue.

Collective Forgiveness

One of the greatest stories of forgiveness we have heard about in recent times occurred on October 2, 2006. Many of us sat stunned before our TV sets, watching the news of a man who had entered a Pennsylvania school, killed five girls ages seven to thirteen and injured five others before turning the gun on himself.

Within hours people began bringing flowers, stuffed toys and signs to leave as a memorial near the school. People were shocked and saddened by the man's horrible, senseless acts. Yet the next day they were also stunned at the news: The children's parents and the entire Amish community announced that they chose to forgive the killer. In fact, they established a fund at a local bank to help his widow and their three young children.

Marie Roberts, widow of the man who pulled the trigger, wrote to them, "I am overwhelmed by the forgiveness, grace and mercy shown to our family. Your love . . . has helped to provide the healing we so desperately need. Please know that we are filled with sorrow for all of our Amish neighbors, whom we have loved and continue to love."

The bloodstained schoolhouse was demolished, but the community continued to put their hope and trust in the God of all comfort as they went about rebuilding their lives.[3]

> When a man's ways please the LORD, He makes even his enemies to be at peace with him.
>
> PROVERBS 16:7

Still another amazing story of forgiveness was in the news in March 2008. A bomb concealed in a gift package and left outside the home of a Christian pastor in Israel exploded when his fifteen-year-old son opened the "gift." The blast, powerful enough to have killed the entire family, critically injured the teenager, who was home alone at the time. Physicians and surgeons treating him called it a miracle that he survived.

In publicly announcing his family's intention to forgive those responsible for the crime, the father said, "If we don't forgive, we become like them . . . we get full of bitterness. Forgiveness is something we do as a favor to ourselves. If God forgives, we also must forgive."[4]

As Pastor Jack Hayford stated in this chapter's opening quote, we should all be thankful to God for His "greatness of grace which looked beyond our faults and . . . totally forgave us." That means all of us! And that same grace is sufficient to free us from any addictions our pain may have driven us to, which we will discuss in the next chapter.

A Prayer to Release Forgiveness

Father, You see my situation and the pain I have suffered because of _____ (name's) words/actions against me. I confess I hold unforgiveness in my heart. I acknowledge this as sin and ask for Your forgiveness and cleansing. Lord, I choose to forgive _____ (name) for _____ (list the offenses), and I release him/ her from my judgment. Please judge _____ (name) according to Your mercy, granting him/her release from bondage. Thank You for the forgiveness I have received. Help me to see _____ (name) as You do and to love him/her with Your love. I ask in Jesus' name, Amen.

6

Lord, I Can't Stop Myself

Do you not know that your body is the temple (the very sanctuary) of the Holy Spirit Who lives within you, Whom you have received [as a Gift] from God? You are not your own, you were bought with a price [purchased with a preciousness and paid for, made His own]. So then, honor God and bring glory to Him in your body.

1 Corinthians 6:19–20, AMP

Because the basic drive in addiction is to avoid painful feelings and experiences, anything that masks these feelings can become an "addictive" cover or escape. Over time, the addictive behavior becomes less effective at blocking the feelings we want to avoid—so we have to ingest the substance or practice the behavior again and again, more and more often, in order to achieve the desired effect. . . . It is here that the potential for sin is very great.

—Dr. Archibald Hart[1]

"Who, me? Hooked? No way!"

Marcia stays in a fog most days as she overdoses on prescription drugs. Frank is a two-pack-a-day smoker. Stacy snacks so often between meals that she has gained seventy pounds in three years. Tony drinks every night after work until he passes out on the couch. Deedra's shopping is out of control, and her credit cards are maxed out. Stan tries to watch every TV sports event possible, to the neglect of his wife and kids.

Not one of these people would admit to being an addict, but each scenario illustrates addictive behavior.

Thinking they can stop at will, people controlled by compulsive behavior do not set out to become addicted. But as they give in to the habit, they soon can find themselves under its control. Whatever activity continually occupies your thoughts and motivates your actions, anything that you "worship," so to speak, can become an addiction. This could be alcohol, street drugs, prescription or over-the-counter drugs, food, shopping, work, exercise or sports, sex, collecting things, housecleaning or even religious activities.

Most addictions are viewed as a controlling desire or need for a substance, object or activity that produces a gratifying reaction. Indulging an addiction may temporarily relax, excite or satisfy you, although you would deny that it controls you. "I can stop anytime I want," the addict tells himself.

But this is the danger of addictions: They become coping mechanisms that remove people from their true feelings of sadness, inadequacy, rejection, anger or pain. Thus these deep emotions remain festering "below the radar" until a crisis brings them boiling to the surface. This was the case with Margarita (see her story in chapter 5), who turned to alcohol to escape painful memories of childhood sexual abuse, until a temporary emotional breakdown put her on a course toward healing.

"I've learned that the thing I depend on in my life controls my life," one recovered drug addict told us. "Therefore I must depend on Jesus Christ." Only after years of addiction that endangered her life and almost caused her to lose custody of her child did the woman in our next story learn this same lesson.

A Downward Spiral

When you first meet Dawn, a beautiful, thirty something brunette, you would never guess she was once hooked on crack cocaine. But she was a woman who could not say no once she turned sixteen and began the downward spiral of smoking, drinking, then venturing into the dark world of illegal drugs. She came from a Christian family—many on her dad's side were pastors. Her substance abuse began in high school, then after she moved away to begin college, her partying increased as she experimented with stronger drugs.

Dawn dropped out of college and moved to a Caribbean island, where her drug use accelerated. When she became pregnant, she married the baby's father and stopped doing drugs during her pregnancy. Although the marriage did not last, she had a precious little daughter. But even moving again did not bring the change Dawn needed.

While Dawn was working as a waitress, someone gave her free crack cocaine. Too weak to resist, she soon was addicted. If she had no money, she would pawn jewelry or anything she could get her hands on just to get a fix. She called the drug her coping mechanism, but her life was quickly spinning out of control.

Finally, Dawn moved back to Florida, told her parents she was a crack addict and entered a four-week rehabilitation center. There, patients were advised to appeal to "a higher power" to help free them of their addictions. The treatment worked at first, and later she married a man she met while in rehab. However, after her release Dawn had a hard time staying clean, and her marriage soon developed problems.

She had a neighbor who was a strong Christian, and as their children played together, the woman talked to Dawn about the Lord. Without being judgmental, the neighbor would pray with her, even when she admitted how heavily involved with drugs she was. Dawn gave her neighbor permission to call her parents if she ever relapsed again.

> But now that you have been set free from sin and have become slaves to God, the benefit you reap leads to holiness, and the result is eternal life.
>
> ROMANS 6:22, NIV

One night after her husband had been arrested and taken to jail, Dawn went partying. When the neighbor called Dawn's mother, she came and took her granddaughter home with her. "I don't think my mom thought she would ever see me alive again," Dawn remembers.

With her daughter and husband gone, she entered a Christian rehab center that offered a year long treatment program. During the first week, she again surrendered her life to the Lord, was baptized in water and quit her abusive habits cold turkey—smoking, drinking and drugs. Dawn stuck with the rigorous spiritual, practical and physical training the facility provided.

"I only saw my child two times that year, when my mother brought her for visits," she said. "One of my goals was to become a loving, responsible mom. I saw many women return to rehab because they fell back into their old habits once they were out. I didn't want that to happen to me.

"When I got out, I felt I should return to my family—the dear ones whom I had humiliated. I had let my life get out of control, but with God's help I determined at the age of twenty-seven never to relapse. I divorced my second husband, went to vocational school, then started working to provide a place for my daughter and me. As a way of giving back, I speak regularly at treatment centers about my long journey out of darkness. Someday I'd like to establish a treatment facility for women struggling as I once did."

Now drug-free for seven years, Dawn tells others that the love of Christ is the only reason for her recovery and sobriety. Today she is an insurance adjuster and mom to her beautiful twelve-year-old daughter. She is married to a Christian man, and they attend church together. What advice would she give someone struggling with substance abuse? She says:

- You have to admit you have a problem, surrender and ask for help. Let go and allow Christ-centered people to assist you through your ordeal.
- You have to commit to a treatment program. I recommend a one-year treatment center. A shorter one didn't work for me, and shorter programs have a higher failure rate.
- You need to get involved with a support group who will hold you accountable, especially when you come out of rehab.
- Avoid driving alone or carrying cash, should you be tempted to drive by your old haunts and buy drugs.
- My lifeline was a Scripture I quoted over and over many times during my recovery days: "I can do all things through Christ who strengthens me" (Philippians 4:13).

Being Responsible

Our human nature often causes us to resort to the "blame game" quickly with regard to our bad habits, just as Adam and Eve did when faced with their sins. Dr. Erwin Lutzer, pastor of the historic Moody Church in Chicago, stresses the importance of believers taking responsibility for their behavior and attitudes. A young man he knew who was addicted to homosexual behavior grew up in a dysfunctional home and came to believe he had been born a homosexual. Dr. Lutzer shares this:

> Is it possible for this man to break free from his sexual addiction? Not if he blames his environment or his genes for his actions. This man did change. Listen to his words: "For years I believed that I could never change because I was a homosexual by constitution, not by choice. I took no responsibility for my behavior. But as I began to read the Scriptures, I began to believe God could change me. The first step in that direction was when I took full responsibility for my behavior. No excuses; no alibis."[2]

Such change in entrenched behavior patterns usually requires a process of several elements: repentance and prayer, personal ministry, Bible study, counseling and the support of a group of believers. But clearly, change is possible.

Those addicted to alcohol, drugs or nicotine become physiologically dependent on the substance, while the dependency on other types of addictions is psychological and emotional. But all addictions have spiritual roots and consequences—the main problem being that they open our minds and emotions to the enemy. In our next story, Faye first thought nothing was wrong with her habit. Then when she decided to quit, she found she could not do it by willpower alone.

A Smoker's Wake-up Call

When Faye was thirty years old, she heard a powerful sermon on how our bodies are the temple of the Holy Spirit.

She had been smoking almost half of her life, but after the message, she went forward and knelt at the altar to give God her cigarette habit.

"Lord, I vow I'll never smoke again; I want to take care of this body You gave me," she prayed.

So she quit—for five whole days. At the time, she was under a great deal of stress: living with an alcoholic husband, holding down a job at a bank and trying to make sure her two young children were cared for. After not working for ten years, she had been forced to find a job because of their financial reverses.

A co-worker who sat next to her at the bank smoked constantly. As the smoke drifted her way, Faye's resistance broke, and she took up the habit again. Besides numbing her pain and relieving the pressure she felt, smoking gave her something to do with her hands. Two days later, when she went dancing with her husband, she suddenly had trouble breathing and began hyperventilating. Panicked, her husband took her to the emergency room.

> If we confess our sins, He is faithful and just to forgive us our sins and to cleanse us from all unrighteousness.
>
> 1 John 1:9

"The medicine they gave me by IV stopped my heart, and my blood pressure dropped so low that I knew I was dying," she told me (Quin). "I heard a doctor say he would try another medication to regulate my heart before applying the paddle. It felt like everything in my body was screaming. In fact, I did scream. Then I saw in my mind a picture of my children, and I knew I wasn't going to die. An indescribable peace enveloped me. It was a landmark spiritual moment as I allowed God to take over."

Suddenly Faye's heart began beating normally on its own. She repented and prayed, "God, I broke my promise to You, and I'm so sorry. Lord, I admit I was in rebellion, but I promise never to smoke again. I truly mean it. Please help me."

That hospital episode changed Faye's outlook about everything and gave her a new hunger for the Lord. She had been a Christian since age nine, but now she felt truly reborn. Once she was released from the hospital and was able to take Communion, God seemed especially real to her. Not long afterward, she began attending a Spirit-filled church despite much opposition from her husband and parents. Then one day alone at home as she sat praying, the Lord baptized her in the Holy Spirit, and she began praising Him with a new prayer language.

Doctors had told Faye she had a leaking heart valve and put her on four different medications. She had never had a heart problem before and could not believe she had one now. Yet when she felt the least pain in her chest, she would become scared because of the frightening diagnosis. One day on her car radio, she heard an evangelist teaching on healing—something very new to her. Did God really heal? As her faith increased, she heard in her mind the Lord's instruction: *Put your hand on your heart and you won't need medicine anymore. You are healed.*

Faye put her hand on her heart and declared, "In Jesus' name I am healed!" An echocardiogram soon showed she had no sign of a leaking heart valve, and she has taken no medicine since that day. Nor has she ever smoked again since making her promise to God in the hospital. "I've been healthy ever since," she said. "What the devil tries to do for evil, God can turn to the good when we submit to Him."

The Enemy's Subtle Trap

We have all heard the old defense "the devil made me do it" when someone tries to excuse his or her bad behavior. Of course the devil cannot force us to do anything, but temptation is his specialty, and we need to be aware of his tactics. Believers become trapped in harmful behavior patterns for a variety of reasons: in an effort to avoid pain, to escape worry, anxiety or confusion, from a need to reduce guilt feelings or from a desire for a perfect self-image.

I (Quin) once interviewed an attractive young woman, a petite size four, who had just won her company's "friendliest employee" award. Renee confessed that five years earlier she was an overweight, matronly looking college graduate, withdrawn and unsociable. For eight years she had struggled with a food disorder known as bulimia.

> For though we walk in the flesh, we do not war according to the flesh. For the weapons of our warfare are not carnal but mighty in God for pulling down strongholds, casting down arguments and every high thing that exalts itself against the knowledge of God, bringing every thought into captivity to the obedience of Christ.
>
> 2 Corinthians 10:3–5

Her mother had always had a weight problem, and when Renee reached puberty, she quickly became self-conscious about her own body image. One afternoon in seventh-grade band practice, she looked down at her thighs and said to herself, *I'm fat*. That day she began believing a lie about herself.

Renee became a "closet eater," secretly snacking on ice cream, candy, doughnuts or pizza, in addition to eating several meals a day. In college she figured out how to use her meal ticket to eat at one dorm, then go to another and eat again. She would swallow up to thirty laxative tablets a day to get the food out of her system.

"I was a perfectionist and a people pleaser, yet I never felt good enough to win the approval of other people," she told me. "I ate a lot to reward myself, as I felt it was the only thing I could have power over. I knew how to time my laxatives after eating to rid myself of the food. But before long the laxatives wouldn't work, then my weight ballooned out of control. I wanted to go out with guys but was afraid of rejection, so in that way my weight protected me."

During summer breaks at home, Renee tried excessive exercise programs—tennis, running, workouts—to prove to herself and her parents that she could lose weight. But back at school, she would begin to binge and purge once again. After eight years of fighting bulimia and its accompanying depression, Renee checked herself into a Christian treatment center for five weeks. She discovered the reasons for her overeating and became accountable to the staff to avoid struggling with her problems alone.

"I'd wanted the perfect figure, the perfect personality, the perfect everything," she said. "Eating had been my selfish pastime. In counseling, I learned to accept myself as God made me. I had to take responsibility for my own choices and stop blaming my parents, my peers or anyone else for the disappointments in my life."

Renee learned biblical principles and concentrated on memorizing Scripture passages. She clung to this verse as her lifeline: "No temptation has overtaken you except such as is common to man; but God is faithful, who will not allow you to be tempted beyond what you are able, but with the temptation will also make the way of escape, that you may be able to bear it" (1 Corinthians 10:13).

Often she prayed, "Lord, provide the way of escape when I'm tempted to overeat." In the ensuing years Renee has kept her weight down, stopped her hateful self-talk and found a reasonable exercise routine. When I attended her storybook wedding, she was radiant. Though she has suffered several miscarriages, she has great faith in God that someday she will have children.

Overeating is one of those "addictions" we usually do not consider wrong. When we are happy, we eat to celebrate. When we are lonely or upset, we eat to comfort ourselves. Dr.

Linda Mintle, a specialist in eating disorders, says we should identify our feelings.

"Are you feeling irritable, bitter, angry, hurt or sorry for yourself? Then make a conscious decision to do something different," she advises. "Take a walk. Listen to music. Work out. Read a book, magazine or newspaper. Or simply take a deep breath and relax your mind."

She suggests making a list of twenty things you can do when you feel upset and are tempted to eat. Put the list on your cupboard, pantry and refrigerator. When you are tempted to reach for food because you are experiencing some troubling emotions, look at the list, then substitute a healthy activity.[3]

This tactic suggested by Dr. Mintle also could help you overcome other types of negative behavior.

Gambling Is a Thief

"I don't see anything in the Bible against gambling," Hal told me (Quin). As a fairly new Christian, he declared he was not ready to give up what he called his "last bad habit."

"There's a lot in the Bible about the right use of your money—or rather God's money," I answered. Then I read him a paraphrased Scripture: "Don't gamble on the pot of gold at the end of the rainbow, hocking your house against a lucky chance. The time will come when you have to pay up; you'll be left with nothing but the shirt on your back" (Proverbs 22:26–27, MESSAGE).

"But I enjoy it—it gives me a way to escape my problems," he joked. "You win a little, lose a little, but it's just fun and exciting."

Hal, like millions of others addicted to this "hidden sickness," has been deceived. Not only had he jeopardized his family's finances, he had lied, bounced checks and tried to conceal the extent of his involvement. When I realized the discussion of his gambling problem was going nowhere, all I could do was to pray that he would come to his senses, repent and get help for his addiction. Gamblers Anonymous support groups are available to help people like Hal.

Compulsive gambling may begin quietly with small amounts of money, but when the gambler wins, his self-image and ego are enhanced. Before long, he is borrowing money to continue gambling in the hope of breaking even. As the compulsion grows, he may give in to lies, loan fraud, absenteeism, family disputes or even a job change as he tries to convince himself that he is about to win big. Such excessive risk-taking adversely affects those closest to him—family members, friends, as well as his employer. It can lead to poor work performance, theft and embezzlement, and can cause the gambler to slip into depression.

Christians are not immune to this habit, and women succumb as well as men—which is a harmful example for their children. In the gym or beauty shop, we have overheard many animated discussions about weekend trips to the casinos or bingo parlors. Of course, the gamblers only brag about their gains, never mentioning their losses. But gambling is a very dangerous form of "entertainment."

The apostle Paul warns us: "The love of money is a root of all kinds of evil, for which some have strayed from the faith in their greediness, and pierced themselves through with many sorrows" (1 Timothy 6:10). If we have indulged in gambling behaviors—even including betting on football game scores in the office pool—maybe we need to pray and reexamine our motives in light of Scripture. Dr. Mark Rutland makes this observation:

> Gambling not only endangers the resources God entrusted into my hands, but also I exploit the passion and lust for

chance in the life of another in order to take his goods with nothing in return. When a state or a nation begins to operate gambling games, it breeds characterlessness and immorality into the lives of its citizenry. The great need in America now is for moral leadership. The end never justifies the means. Do not be fooled by how many textbooks a state lottery will buy.[4]

Obsession with Video Games

Millions of children and adults in our nation are obsessed with playing video games, prompting some doctors to consider calling it an addiction. One physician raised the concern due to reports that people are losing their social contacts because of overuse of video games. He says video gaming is not unlike alcohol or gambling addictions because it is having a profound negative impact on individuals and families.[5]

The typical "addict" is a thirty-year-old male who spends seven to eight hours a week gaming, according to a software association. One survey found that video game overuse was most prevalent among users who play against others in massive role-playing games on the Internet.

While more and more adults are pursuing their social relationships in a virtual reality realm rather than in real-life encounters, statistics show that far too many children are doing the same thing. They spend

> Be self-controlled and alert. Your enemy the devil prowls around like a roaring lion looking for someone to devour. Resist him, standing firm in the faith.
>
> 1 Peter 5:8–9, NIV

a disproportionate amount of time on video games that are often loaded with violent imagery and can lead to aggressive behavior. One estimate says that up to 90 percent of American children play video games. Two-thirds of parents surveyed reported that they were very concerned about sex and violence their children are exposed to via the media and video gaming.[6]

Video game dangers are many: viewing violent scenes, occult involvement, expressing rage when losing, plus wasting valuable time and isolating oneself from family and friends. The Bible says we are to avoid "the lust of the flesh, the lust of the eyes, and the pride of life" because they are worldly and not of the Father (see 1 John 2:16).

Tommy is a father whose two-year obsession with video games consumed his thought life. Many nights while his family slept, he would sneak down to his computer in the basement and play games, many of which were occultic. The following day, he would brag to co-workers and his teenage son about his gaming ability, but he was usually sleepy and mean-spirited.

Then Tommy became a Christian and decided to completely destroy his game collection so he would not have to deal with the temptation. He asked his wife to help him smash his games. Here is what he said about his recovery:

- I admitted to myself and to God that I was addicted. I hadn't realized the hold the occult had on me, or that God forbids it in Scripture. I asked for and received God's forgiveness.

- I wanted my wife to be involved in the process of destroying my games, as she had been warning me for months of the dangers. I wanted her to hold me accountable.

- I had to guard myself when tempted to try fantasy football gaming or other online offers.

- Now I play board games with my children after supper. We talk about strategies in winning the fun games we enjoy and strategies for living life God's way.

Compulsive Shopping

Francine was so obsessed with bargain hunting that for years she spent most of her office lunch breaks window shopping instead of eating. On weekends she generally went mall hopping in search of bargains. When she quit her job and her husband neared retirement, she realized she was truly addicted and began seeking God's help.

To stay free, Francine always prays before going shopping, asking God to help her avoid temptation and be wise and prudent in her purchases. She determines in advance not to do any impulse buying, but to get only the items on her shopping list. And she is careful to stay within her specified budget.

Another addicted shopper told us the only way she got free was to cut up her credit cards, then ask her husband or a friend to go shopping with her until she could resist temptations enough to shop alone again.

We need to remember that addictions have spiritual consequences. Our human nature is basically rebellious and self-centered. Addictive behavior, to put it bluntly, is spiritual idolatry that keeps us depending on things for satisfaction, rather than relying on a loving God.

"I'm on a greater high with the Lord than I ever got on alcohol—and I never have a hangover the next day!" a former alcoholic who was freed from her bondage told us. "I gave Him my addiction, and He gave me freedom and a new life."

If, after reading this chapter, you feel an addiction has you in such dark bondage that you will never see the light, do not believe that lie. "There is no pit so deep but that Jesus' love is deeper still," Corrie ten Boom used to say. God is always there to deliver you and help you recover. Just turn to Him by praying the following prayer.

PRAYER

Lord, only You can give me the strength I need to overcome this huge problem that has gripped me in my weakest area. I acknowledge that my addiction is displeasing to You and is a snare in my Christian walk. I confess that in the past, I have enjoyed it and have been unwilling to lay it down, but I truly desire to overcome it. I don't want to remain a slave to this sin of _____ (name addiction). Thank You in advance that You'll enable me to walk free of this unholy habit. I ask in Jesus' name, Amen.

7

Lord, Help Me
Stop Taking Control

If you give encouraging guidance, be careful that you don't get bossy; if you're put in charge, don't manipulate; if you're called to give aid to people in distress, keep your eyes open and be quick to respond; if you work with the disadvantaged, don't let yourself get irritated with them or depressed by them. Keep a smile on your face.

Romans 12:6–8, MESSAGE

Manipulation is a crafty use of the tongue and a self-perpetuating vice. Once manipulators find that their craftiness helps them to achieve their objectives, they become proud of their "smooth operation" skills. They will use all kinds of indirect tactics ranging from "guilt trips" to portraying themselves as innocent, suffering victims of various circumstances. They may even start to enjoy their ability to influence others in such a manner.

—Deborah Smith Pegues[1]

Have you ever felt intimidated by someone—a boss, perhaps —and realized that this person was manipulating you? Yet you did not know what to do about it. Very often the person doing the manipulating has authority over you and uses it to maintain control. Or in your honest moments, have you ever acknowledged that you were the one trying to control a person or situation?

Such exploitation is a tactic people use to try to get what they want from others. People who are controlling exhibit self-ish motives by seeking to get their own needs met, but many fail to recognize this trait either in themselves or in others. The behavior is totally opposite of our Christian mandate to serve, not be served. Jesus said, "Whoever desires to become great among you shall be your servant" (Mark 10:43).

Manipulation is not God's will. He does not employ such tactics to force us to choose His ways—He gives us freedom of choice. And He does not want us to manipulate others for our own selfish reasons.

Most of us have met control freaks who try to micromanage everything around them. Often they are motivated by some type of fear, usually a fear of rejection. Perhaps they experienced abandonment, neglect or abuse during childhood, and they do not intend to be hurt or rejected again. Perhaps their low self-esteem or unstable economic situation causes them to feel insecure and inferior, so their controlling behavior is their way of compensating.

Parents sometimes attempt to manipulate their married children, even to dictating where they spend the holidays. "If you don't come home for Christmas, just don't come home at all," has been expressed on occasion. Some make extravagant offers with strings attached. "I'll send you to college if you promise to help send your younger brothers to college," a father told his oldest daughter. "No thanks, Dad. I'll work for my own tuition, just like they can work for theirs," she told him.

I (Ruthanne) know of Christian parents who became angry when they learned one of their children volunteered to serve on the mission field in another part of the world. One woman even said to me, "I told my daughter and her husband they can go if they want to, but they have to leave my grandkids here!" She said it in a joking manner, but I could see she really was struggling with the issue.

Naturally, most of us would prefer having our kids and grandkids living close to home. But Scripture teaches that we should offer ourselves to God as an act of worship (see Romans 12:1), and for some this may mean accepting a work or ministry assignment a great distance from their family home. Not only should we parents be willing to serve the Lord wherever He may call us, we should allow our children the liberty to do the same.

> Let love be without hypocrisy. Abhor what is evil. Cling to what is good. Be kindly affectionate to one another with brotherly love, in honor giving preference to one another.
>
> ROMANS 12:9–10

While young children are growing and developing, of course, parents should nurture, guide and protect them from harmful influences. This means controlling their environment for a season until they are mature enough to make decisions on their own and deal with the results. But eventually children must learn to accept the consequences of their own choices.

I recall a time when I (Ruthanne) was worried that my son might fail his eleventh-grade algebra course. His marks had been dropping throughout the semester. My response was to arrange a time for him to meet with a tutor to prepare for his final exam, but this headstrong seventeen-year-old refused to go.

One day I was praying a paraphrased version of Isaiah 54:13: "Thank You that my son will be taught of the Lord, and great will be his peace." Immediately the Lord spoke these words to my heart: *If you want Me to be his teacher, then you must get out of the way.*

Difficult as it was, I knew I had to stop trying to protect my stubborn child from his own poor choices. I needed to allow him to learn his lesson the hard way. I cancelled the appointment with the tutor, and my son barely passed that algebra course. A year later, he reaped the consequences when his top-choice university rejected his application. Later God graciously opened another door of opportunity for him to study architecture, and the Lord has continued to be my son's teacher throughout the years. For me as a parent, it was a lesson in letting go of control and trusting God with the outcome.

An overprotective parent's behavior not only stifles a child's creativity and hinders his or her development, but also sometimes leads to estrangement between the parent and child. The following story illustrates one aspect of this problem.

A Controlling Mother

Dot, a friend of mine (Quin's), is an example of someone who refused to be manipulated by a controlling family member.

Adopted as an infant by a maternal aunt, Dot was grown before she learned that the woman she had always called Aunt Marie actually was her birth mother. Soon after Dot learned the truth about her birth, this "aunt" wanted to establish a mother-daughter relationship with her. Though Dot and her husband had moved far away, she would try to write interesting things about her children to Aunt Marie. But for a response, she would get back pages of instructions on how she should raise the kids. If she sent a birthday or Christmas gift, Aunt Marie rarely liked it.

"My parents were good to me," Dot said. "They fed me, clothed me and gave me a loving home. How could I suddenly allow another woman to try taking the place of my mom when she didn't have anything constructive to add to my life or family? The poor dear was a cross old lady, very hard to get along with. I just couldn't acknowledge her as my mother."

Dot chose not to let Aunt Marie's selfish desires and attitudes control her life. But she and her husband prayed for her and remembered her with gifts on special occasions, feeling this should be the extent of their involvement in her life.

> But the wisdom that is from above is first pure, then peaceable, gentle, willing to yield, full of mercy and good fruits, without partiality and without hypocrisy.
>
> JAMES 3:17

One year while attending a relative's funeral back in her home state, Dot decided to go see Aunt Marie at the nursing home where she lived. She convinced her cousin Shirley to go along.

Though they wanted to visit Aunt Marie in a private room, the elderly lady insisted she would just stay put in the public lounge area. As they talked, the man sitting nearby listened in on their conversation. Aunt Marie asked Shirley, "What church do you belong to?" Upon her response, Marie said, "I belong to that denomination, too."

Dot spoke up and said, "Aunt Marie, it doesn't matter which church you belong to. What really counts is whether or not you've invited Jesus to come live in your heart—to be your Lord."

As quickly as those words were spoken, Aunt Marie replied, "I accept Jesus as my personal Savior."

The man sitting next to her said, "And so do I."

The Holy Spirit had prepared Marie's heart, and this visit was the catalyst for her to receive Christ.

"Two souls came into God's Kingdom that day," Dot said. "I never saw Aunt Marie again—she fell and broke her hip and died the following year. But I'm grateful for the opportunity God gave me to reach out to her."

While Dot had firmly stood against allowing Aunt Marie to maintain a hold on her life, God used her years of prayer and her personal visit to change this woman's life.

A "Jezebel Spirit"

"She's just a Jezebel," people often say when describing a controlling person. This idolatrous queen corrupted her husband, King Ahab, as well as the rest of Israel, leading them to worship the pagan god Baal. Jezebel would stop at nothing when she made up her mind to get what she wanted. Even the prophet Elijah fled from her death threats after God had helped him to destroy her false prophets. When Ahab wanted his neighbor Naboth's vineyard, Jezebel arranged for false charges to be brought against the man. He was stoned to death, then Ahab took the vineyard (see 1 Kings 18:20–39; 19:1–3; 21:5–16).

A person with a controlling spirit such as Jezebel had can be either male or female, and you will find such people in all walks of life. A friend of ours, Alicia, told us how she was both deceived and manipulated by someone whom she greatly admired—a woman with an established ministry.

> Do nothing out of selfish ambition or vain conceit, but in humility consider others better than yourselves. Each of you should look not only to your own interests, but also to the interests of others.
>
> PHILIPPIANS 2:3-4, NIV

After Alicia had graduated from Bible school, this minister told her, "I feel that God wants you to work with me." Even though she could not get a clear direction from the Lord about the invitation, Alicia finally gave in to the pressure and moved to another city to join the woman's staff. When she discovered the ministry did not intend to pay her a salary, she had to find part-time work to cover living expenses.

Soon the woman minister was controlling almost every aspect of Alicia's life, constantly telling her what to do—but still Alicia did not discern the deception and control. During a ministry trip to another city, some of Alicia's friends came to the meeting.

"They saw how I was being controlled and afterward tried to warn me that I needed to leave that ministry, but their advice offended me," Alicia admitted.

Her friends met and prayed together for two hours that Alicia's eyes would be opened to truth. One friend then talked to her again. "Alicia, because of that woman's control over you, your personality has changed—you're not even the same person you used to be," she said.

Finally, Alicia's spiritual eyes were opened. She left the ministry, returned to her former city and found a new job. "I learned I must always receive a word from the Lord for myself and not listen to what other people say is God's will for me—even those high up in ministry," she shared. "I'm glad my friends cared enough about me to pray and then confront me with the truth about my deception."

Sad to say, Alicia's experience is not that uncommon. No doubt you can think of someone in your own circle of friends or family who tries to control others through guilt, intimidation, criticism, condescension, threats or abuse of power. A few controllers and their targets whom we know about include:

- Darlene, the charge nurse in a large city hospital, who terrorized those she supervised by yelling at them for the slightest mistake, real or imagined. She demanded total control of the thermostat for the entire floor, with no regard for the comfort of patients or anyone else. After workers lodged many complaints against her, Darlene's boss transferred her to another position, afraid to fire her for fear she would sue the hospital.

- Martha, who married a widower with two very spoiled children. He told her, "If you can't love my children as your own, we won't have any children together." And they never did, though she longed to have a baby of her own. She showered love on both her stepdaughters, but they never called her "Mom" until they reached adulthood.

- Brenda, a strong-willed sixteen-year-old, who tried all the wrong ways to be the center of attention in her family of five. She climbed out her bedroom window at night to meet a boyfriend, experimented with drugs and shoplifted cosmetics. Her upper-middle-class parents kept rescuing her, even though they realized she was manipulating them with her wrong choices. Finally, they sent her away to boarding school.

- Harry, who chose a teaching career he did not like just to please his mom. Often he told his math students that he hated his job, wanting instead to make things with his hands. But his mother held Harry captive by telling him she had paid for his college training to be a teacher, and he felt he just could not let her down.

Passivity: A Form of Control?

Can someone whose behavior is passive be a controller? Yes, says Ann, a believer who longed for a picture-perfect marriage but found herself married to Troy, who seemed stuck in passive mode. Guess who had to change? Ann tells us her story:

One day we drove home from church in a lightly falling rain. As soon as we walked into the living room, I screamed, "Troy, look at this water dripping through the ceiling. Do something!"

"Oh, you can call the roof repairman tomorrow," he said as he glanced at the puddles on the hardwood floor and plopped down on the sofa to read the Sunday paper. I climbed up into the attic and spread out sheets of plastic to catch the water coming through the roof. Once more, his indifference and passivity made me boil.

We never fought—Troy simply would withdraw and refuse to address the issue at hand. Conflict resolution was never modeled for him as he grew up, and his attitude was that in time everything would take care of itself. Why couldn't he be like husbands in the storybook marriages I'd read about?

I loved Troy, but often I really didn't like him. I dreamed of a marriage where he was not so aloof. He's a righteous, stable, professional man, highly esteemed by his patients and friends. He has a marvelous sense of humor that often embarrasses me. But he lived out of his sense of logic, while my emotions ruled me. When our children were young, they depended on him for fun, trips, family games and support in all their activities. Since most of their discipline was left up to me, it seemed I was always the "heavy."

Sometimes I felt I had another child on my hands—my own husband! Periodically I'd indulge in episodes of crying and demand the love and attention I thought I deserved. But Troy would just retreat further into passivity. "Help, God!" became my frequent cry, which really meant, "God, change this man." The more I tried to move him to action, the more he resisted. *Can't he carry out the garbage just once a week without being reminded?* I'd fume silently.

Over and over I went around my mountain of impatience with Troy, judging and criticizing in my heart. I'd pray and get a measure of victory, then I'd fall right back into chafing over his actions or lack of action. I knew this wasn't God's ideal for a Christian wife. My heavenly Father lavished love on me in spite of my failures and shortcomings—shouldn't I do the same for my own husband?

> You are still controlled by your sinful nature. You are jealous of one another and quarrel with each other. Doesn't that prove you are controlled by your sinful nature? Aren't you living like people of the world?
>
> 1 CORINTHIANS 3:3, NLT

While reading Mike Mason's *The Mystery of Marriage*, I was deeply convicted that I should stop trying to re-create my husband in an image I had for him. I needed to let go of wanting him to come into line with my expectations. Instead, I began to look for and appreciate the unique person that Troy truly is, focus on his many good qualities and compliment him on those.

I've determined not to let Troy manipulate me because of my insecurities and my need to feel loved and appreciated. I now address issues without accusing him or assigning blame, and I take responsibility for my attitudes when they get out of control.

Did our lives change? Yes. As I lived out this concept of trying to see Troy as God made him, it was like letting a bird out of a cage. He began moving closer to me emotionally, and now he is free to be the man God created him to be. I may not agree with the way he does everything, but most of the time I can just let it float by.

These days when we have a household emergency, he actually helps out. We laugh a lot about our differences. Also, I now admit that sometimes it's better to be passive. My previous attitude was "Do something!"—even if what he did was wrong. I made many mistakes by rushing headlong into situations when I should have waited for God's guidance. Now

I sometimes sit back and just wait and wait and wait until my husband moves, but I can do it without getting upset.

Ann's story illustrates how marriages and interpersonal relationships suffer harm when one insecure, passive person tries to control the behavior of others. We need to be aware of how the enemy uses this human weakness to create discord and dissension in families, and we need to confess and repent for our own controlling tendencies when necessary.

Control versus Conviction

The silent treatment is a form of control a person may exert by cutting off all communication with someone who has offended him or her. I (Quin) knew a husband who got mad at his wife for buying household furniture without asking his advice on color or style, so he refused to speak to her for over a year! It was terribly uncomfortable to be in their home during that time.

You probably know someone who has tried every way possible to "make" his or her spouse become a believer. But the control tactics did not work and probably alienated the mate even further. One of the Holy Spirit's roles is to convict of sin and draw a person to the Lord. Our part is to pray for our mates, allow Christ's character to be seen in us and trust God to do the rest. Above all, we cannot tell God how and when to answer our prayers.

God approaches each individual in a personal way—He does not work according to human methods or timetables (see Isaiah 55:8–9). If there is anything we need as wives or husbands, it is patience to wait for a spouse to join us on the believers' bench. Meanwhile, it is important to remember we are always accountable to God for our own behavior.

Joan was a homemaker in her late twenties and married with two children when she became a Christian. Naturally, she wanted her husband to follow her.

"Accepting Jesus totally transformed my life," she told us. "In fact, my husband felt he scarcely knew this strange woman he was now living with! But to my dismay, Stuart had no interest in sharing my experience." Joan began to pray, but nothing seemed to change. Then the Lord spoke three things to her:

1. *Let Me show you how to love your husband with unconditional love—just the way I love him.*
2. *I want you to pray that your husband will become the man of God that I, the Lord, desire to see—not the man you are wanting to see.*
3. *Pursue Me with all your heart. Don't wait for your husband to share your interest in spiritual matters.*

"With the Lord's help, I began following His instructions," Joan said. "I stopped trying to manipulate Stuart into changing his behavior. I released him completely for the Lord to work in his life. And my own life was completely fulfilled, because I was having such a wonderful time getting acquainted with Jesus."

One day Stuart told Joan he was going to the Gulf on a fishing trip. This had often been a source of conflict because she did not like fishing and thought he spent too much time at it. But this day, she just waved him off with, "That's fine, Honey—have a good time." He could tell she was sincere because she had stopped nagging him.

Over the next five years, Joan saw a gradual change as her husband grew closer to the Lord. In the meantime, she guarded herself from acting so superspiritual that he felt put down. She saw the Lord change her husband into a loving, compassionate man of God—a far greater work than she could have dreamed possible. He not only became a godly role model for their sons, but a wonderful husband to Joan. Today they are in ministry together.

Joan's experience reminds us that praying for God to intervene in our loved ones' lives is a powerful tool. He invites us to "come boldly to the throne of grace, that we may obtain mercy and find grace to help in time of need" (Hebrews 4:16). Once we bring Him our petitions, though, we must leave the timing and method of the answer in His hands. We are to submit to His Lordship—not pray controlling prayers in an attempt to manipulate circumstances or another person's behavior.

Elisabeth Elliot writes:

> Is it our business to pry into what may happen tomorrow? It is a difficult and painful exercise which saps the strength and uses up the time given us today. Once we give ourselves up to God, shall we attempt to get hold of what can never belong to us—tomorrow? Our lives are His, our times in His hand. He is Lord over what *will* happen, never mind what may happen. When we prayed "Thy will be done," did we suppose He did not hear us? . . . If my life is once surrendered, all is well. Let me not grab it back, as though it were in peril in His hand but would be safer in mine![2]

Overcontrolling Father

One of the saddest examples of overcontrolling we have read about occurred in nineteenth-century England. You have no doubt read the poem containing the famous lines, "How do I love thee? Let me count the ways." Renowned poet Elizabeth Barrett, who penned them, was one of twelve children. Her tyrannical father, Edward, forbade any of his children to marry. When Elizabeth secretly married Robert Browning in 1846, her father disowned her. After their marriage, the Brownings sailed for Italy, where they lived for the rest of their lives.

Elizabeth wrote letters to her father almost weekly, but he never replied. After ten years, she received a large box in the mail containing those letters—all unopened. Today those messages written by a loving daughter to an overcontrolling father are considered among the most beautiful in classical English literature. If only Elizabeth's dad had read a few, perhaps their relationship would have been restored. But reportedly, he had such a desire to control his family that he also disinherited the other two children who chose to marry.[3]

We all wish this story had a happy ending, but it did not. Today many families are no doubt likewise suffering from one member's domineering power and control over the others. One wife we know, Carmen, found herself in this dilemma and also found a way to solve it.

Carmen was frustrated when her husband, Steve, berated her and demanded she act in a certain way. She kept asking God how she should respond. God gave her wisdom, and the next time Steve yelled commands at her, she replied, "This behavior is really beneath you, Steve. I know you're a loving, caring man—the same sweet, gentle man I married years ago. I choose not to be manipulated." In time he changed his attitude and behavior toward her.

"If you are struggling as I was, ask God to give you a willing heart to love unconditionally, but the wisdom to set proper boundaries," Carmen said. "I had to remember how God valued and loved me, and that I couldn't expect to gain my full sense of value from my husband. Only God can give me that."

We asked several people, "What rubs you the wrong way about people who are controlling?" Here are some of their answers:

- They almost always make you feel bad, as if an awkward situation is your fault when it's really theirs.
- They may repeatedly tell lies and don't seem to care about the rights of others.
- They're consistently unpredictable.
- Most of the time, they don't accept responsibility for anything they've done unless it's something they can brag about.
- Manipulative people thrive on attention, even negative attention.

Now the question we may need to ask ourselves is, "Am I a controlling person? If so, how do I overcome this detrimental habit?"

> Just say "yes" and "no." When you manipulate words to get your own way, you go wrong.
>
> MATTHEW 5:37, MESSAGE

Though this may be one of the hardest habits to break, if your answer is yes, here are some suggestions:

- Recognize and admit your controlling tendencies.
- Ask God to help you overcome the habit.
- Learn to say "I'm sorry."
- Be accountable to someone who will be honest enough to tell you when you are trying to control a person or situation.

When Paul wrote, "The love of God has been poured out in our hearts by the Holy Spirit who was given to us" (Romans 5:5), he was speaking about a love that seeks the highest good of the other person, a self-giving love, the kind of unconditional love God has for us.[4] At those times when we ask for the Holy Spirit's help, we discover we can become conduits through which God's love will flow to others.

As we have seen throughout this chapter, manipulation is a damaging and unhealthy way to influence and interact with others. Let's ask God to help us guard our tongues and actions in all our relationships.

Resisting the temptation to scheme to fulfill our own desires will help us purify our hearts. And this is the topic we will look at in the next chapter.

PRAYERS

If you tend to manipulate others, pray the following:

Heavenly Father, I repent for the times I've tried to control the behavior of those close to me, and I ask for Your forgiveness. Instead of controlling others myself, I determine to allow You to control me. Please draw _____ (name) to You and help me respond and relate to (him/her) in the right way with the right words, without manipulation. Help me relinquish all control to the Holy Spirit, I ask in Jesus' name, Amen.

If you tend to allow others to manipulate you, pray this prayer:

Dear Lord, help me learn how to avoid allowing others to manipulate me into doing things I know are wrong or things I don't want to do. I choose to forgive the motives and actions of those who have attempted to control me. I know it's not Your will for me to be a doormat, yet I sometimes feel intimidated by people and hesitant about voicing my opinion. Give me wisdom and boldness to take a stand so that others don't take advantage of me. Thank You for helping me, Lord. Amen.

8

Lord, Purify My Heart

Keep your heart with all diligence, for out of it spring the issues of life.

Proverbs 4:23

Flee also youthful lusts; but pursue righteousness, faith, love, peace with those who call on the Lord out of a pure heart.

2 Timothy 2:22

When the Holy Spirit quickens our spirit as we believe, repent, and receive the gospel, we are spiritually transformed. This transformation includes a revelation of our sin-guilt and our hopelessness apart from Christ's saving grace. . . . Once we are saved, it is our responsibility to discipline our bodies and souls to bring them into line with God's truth as revealed in His Word.

—Alice Smith[1]

Most of us, if we are truthful, admit that we need God's help to keep our hearts pure. Whether we are grappling to overcome envy, sexual temptation, judging, gossip, prejudice, pride or any number of bad habits, we desperately need His power to achieve victory.

We are well aware that sexual temptation is rampant in society today, and Christians certainly are not immune from the struggle. In recent years, we have seen the moral standard for what is appropriate content for magazines, television programs, advertising, movies and the Internet drop to an all-time low. In the name of "free speech," our culture is saturated with sexual messages through all sorts of media, making pornography easily accessible even for children.

Not only are pornography and its accompanying problems corrupting our nation, they are crippling the Church. In one report, 57 percent of pastors said that addiction to pornography is the most sexually damaging issue to their congregations.[2]

According to a Focus on the Family poll, 47 percent of families listed pornography as a problem they face. In yet another survey, 54 percent of pastors polled admitted they had viewed Internet pornography within that year. Revenues of the sex and porn industry in the United States were reportedly 13.3 billion dollars in 2006.[3]

Curiosity Got the Best of Him

One Christian husband reported that he began viewing porn out of curiosity. After being bombarded almost daily with emails and advertisements for Internet sex, he decided one day to click onto one of the ads just to see what it was about. He was shocked and outraged by the raw images provided free of charge. Immediately he exited the site, but the next day he went back. He clicked and looked again. Afterward the fantasies played over and over in his mind, even after he stopped watching.

Yes, he knew what he was doing was wrong. He wondered what he would say to his children if he were caught. How would his wife feel? What would happen to his reputation as a Christian if his friends knew? He decided he must stop, and he spent time confessing his sin to the Lord. Then by installing a filtering device on his computer to block the porn sites, he closed the door on porn addiction and avoided being taken over by it. Although he was ashamed about having even experimented with watching such filth, he now shares his own experience as a way to help other men get free.

> Do not love or cherish the world or the things that are in the world. If anyone loves the world, love for the Father is not in him.
>
> For all that is in the world—the lust of the flesh [craving for sensual gratification] and the lust of the eyes [greedy longings of the mind] and the pride of life [assurance in . . . the stability of earthly things]—these do not come from the Father but are from the world [itself].
>
> And the world passes away.
>
> 1 John 2:15–17, AMP

Another man admitted to a seven-year addiction, which went on even while he regularly attended a secular program for sexual addicts. He thinks it took way too long for his healing. No one in the program told him about his need for Christ's forgiveness, nor that God would accept him in spite of his imperfections. A heart-to-heart encounter with the Lord, as well as a commitment to be accountable to certain friends, helped him get delivered and find his way to freedom.

Pastor Ted Roberts was a forerunner in offering counseling and small group ministry to those struggling with sex addictions at his Oregon church. He says that many who come for counseling have repented innumerable times and tried everything they know of to follow Christ. But they are trapped.

He describes addiction as "deciding not to do something and finding yourself not only doing it, but getting worse."

His church is dedicated to walking with an addict—however long it takes—until the person attains freedom. He further writes:

> Addicts must address their sense of worthlessness at the point of their shame. They have to find a safe place where they can finally let all the secrets out—with nothing held back. Small group ministry [through churches] is a critical key in this process. Without it we can never come to a place of confessing our sins to one another in order to be healed (see James 5:16). Obviously, confidentiality and careful structuring of the groups are essential. This process of breaking the addicted mind-set is never a quick-fix process. . . . Our goal is getting healthy, not just stopping destructive behavior. And that will probably take three to five years, with the Holy Spirit doing miracles all along as they cooperate.[4]

Many Christians expect the Lord to deal with their problem miraculously. Roberts says that while God does move in that way, the process of healing involves renewing one's mind, which does not happen overnight. The recovering addict has to cooperate, and one of the most challenging steps is for him or her to learn to walk in God's grace.

I (Quin) was visiting a church in Virginia years ago when the pastor gave an unusual altar call: "All men who want to be free of addiction to pornography, please come to the altar for prayer." As at least sixty men left their seats and walked forward, I knew it took great courage for them to be vulnerable in front of their families and friends. The pastor gave a powerful deliverance-type prayer, then asked them to sign up for counseling and support groups that he was starting. Would that every church offered such a haven of healing for this issue and other related addictions!

The Entire Family Suffers Loss

Sometime later, Ruthanne and I interviewed a woman whose marriage had been destroyed by her husband's twenty-year addiction to pornography. She told us of the insidious ways a wife is made to feel that the problem is really her fault—by her husband and sometimes even by well-meaning counselors. The "if only" syndrome fills her mind with false guilt:

If only I could be better in bed. . . . If only I could find out what pleases him. . . . What is it about me he doesn't like? . . . If only I could lose weight and get in shape. . . . If only I could do better preparing meals and keeping house. . . . If only I could make him proud of me. . . .

This wife went to four Christian counselors and two different pastors to seek help, but none could understand her dilemma. After repeatedly being told she should go home and be more submissive, she came away broken and doubting her own sanity.

At one time her husband had been a brilliant engineer in corporate management. But over the years, after becoming incapable of thinking clearly or solving even simple problems due to his mental preoccupation with pornography, he was reduced to a low-paying job on a production line. So extreme was his fantasizing that he could not even carry on a conversation at the dinner table. His wife and children became victims of his addiction. Sadly, when he became physically abusive, she went into hiding for her own safety.

> Create in me a clean heart, O God,
> And renew a steadfast spirit within me.
> Do not cast me away from Your presence,
> And do not take Your Holy Spirit from me.
>
> PSALM 51:10–11

Over the years, women we have interviewed who faced this problem suggest a wife should look for these signs as clues that her husband is addicted: He may resist being drawn into conversation or seem sullen at the dinner table. He may stare into space, lost in a fantasyland of his imagination. He may begin criticizing you for being overweight, for the way you dress or for not meeting his needs. You may dread going to bed at night for fear of what he may demand of you.

If there is any evidence he has visited prostitutes, you should also be tested for sexually transmitted diseases and take precautions to protect yourself.

Jesus gave this warning: "Your eye is a lamp that provides light for your body. When your eye is good, your whole body is filled with light. But when your eye is bad, your whole body is filled with darkness" (Matthew 6:22–23, NLT). The enemy is still using the eye gate to draw his victims into darkness, and pornography is a powerful avenue more easily accessed today than ever before.

Confrontation Is Necessary

A few months after my (Quin's) friend Jody got married, she found her husband's hidden pornographic magazines. She considered leaving Rex right then. But she rededicated her life to the Lord and began praying for her marriage to be healed. Although Rex promised to get rid of his stash when she confronted him, their intimate times were stressful.

After discovering his hidden porn for the third time, Jody gave him an ultimatum: "Either you agree to get help and become accountable to a godly man, or I'm leaving you, Rex—I really mean it this time."

Rex realized she was serious and his marriage could be over. That evening, he confessed his problem to his pastor and repented before the Lord. The pastor led him in a deliverance prayer, and Rex commanded the spirit of lust to release him in the name of Jesus. After Rex's long session with the pastor, Jody and Rex's marriage gradually began changing for the better until it was restored.

Jody has advice for other wives: "Confront your husband the first time the problem is exposed, and be forceful about his choice. I believe by putting off the confrontation, it took much longer for me to receive healing for myself and to be able to trust my husband again. Confront and set boundaries. Let your husband know there will be consequences when his behavior is unacceptable."

We advise women to seek the Lord for wise strategy on how to broach this volatile subject. If God allows you to discover such a problem with your husband, He will give you directions on how to deal with it appropriately. The goal is to see your spouse restored and your marriage strengthened.

Women Beware

Women, too, can become ensnared in sexual fantasies and be vulnerable to affairs, especially through cyberspace. Christian teacher Judy Reamer talks about mental adultery, which can be a problem for singles as well as for married women. She says,

> Whether your source of sexual temptation is an old boyfriend, a man on the job, or only someone you have had a dream about, the solution is still the same. . . . Improper sexual behavior always starts first in the mind. . . . Therefore, while this solution may sound simplistic—it is still the best answer: STOP THE THOUGHTS! Nip them in the bud. . . . Do not let your imagination run away from you.
>
> Choose not to review last night's passionate dream. Occupy your mind with organizing your day. Read the Bible, listen to a program on a Christian radio station, or dig out a new recipe for supper. Before long, the sexual thoughts will

dissipate. . . . Remember my little motto, "Affairs start in the head before they get to the bed."[5]

When a believer allows herself to come under the deception that Internet liaisons are harmless, Satan can use the resulting immorality to destroy her relationship with God. Most of us have heard of someone who left family and everything else for an unknown stranger whom she (or he) met in an Internet chat room. Some preachers have fallen prey to this tactic when the enemy caused them to become fascinated with a new and exciting person who seemed so desirable.

The truth is that no human relationship—whether with a spouse or anyone else—can totally fulfill our emotional and spiritual needs. Only a vital relationship with Christ can equip us to establish healthy ties with family members and others in our lives. No person can fill the God-shaped void in our spirit that can be satisfied only by our Creator.

Too Easily Deceived

Lucy fell into a trap of deception at church, of all places. For three years she was involved in a prayer team ministry composed of one man, another woman and herself. Two nights a week they met at church to pray for two or three hours for people with great needs. After a while, Lucy realized she felt attracted to the man on her team. She would pray to get rid of impure thoughts and then be fine for a while, but the thoughts would come back.

"I was repulsed and attracted at the same time," she told me (Quin). "I knew it was wrong, but I enjoyed our wonderful evenings of prayer. I began to prefer being there to staying at home with my husband." Then she got a wake-up call when she dreamed she and the man were in church together and he asked her for a date. In the dream, Lucy looked behind the pulpit and saw Jesus with an agonized look on His face. Mocking demons lurked in the dark behind Him.

"In an instant, this dream showed me how much Jesus loved me and suffered for me," she said. "My heart was broken as I saw He wanted me to have a pure life. I knew I needed to repent, to completely turn away from lustful thoughts at all costs. I knew He was saying, 'Break up the prayer team into men praying with men and women praying with women.'"

> Finally, brethren, whatever things are true, whatever things are noble, whatever things are just, whatever things are pure, whatever things are lovely, whatever things are of good report, if there is any virtue and if there is anything praiseworthy—meditate on these things.
>
> PHILIPPIANS 4:8

Lucy wept and repented, asking God's forgiveness. Then she told her male prayer partner she would no longer pray on his team, and he agreed it would be for the best. Later she learned this turned his marriage around—his wife had felt left out and inferior because she was not part of the prayer group.

Lucy still was not happy with her marriage, especially when she compared her quiet husband with the outgoing man whose company she had so enjoyed. The turning point came when she and her spouse attended a conference together. Lying beside him in bed one night, she prayed, *Lord, please break the sound barrier between my husband and me.* She heard one word: *Amen.*

"I didn't know if it was an angel or God speaking," she said. "But I was profoundly touched by a hope I'd never had before, and I knew God was healing my heart and my marriage."

Over the next year, her love grew as the two developed a real bonding. Her husband did not talk more, read less, watch TV less or stop doing the things that used to irritate her. But God had enlarged her heart toward him and given her the grace to walk out of a potentially dangerous relationship.

Like Lucy, we all have vulnerable areas where we need to guard against falling into temptation. However, sexual sins are not the only ones that cause us to have an impure heart.

Other Impurities

Paul warned the Galatians about the "works of the flesh" such as adultery, fornication and lewdness. Yet in the same passage he included hatred, wrath, envy, idolatry and dissensions, all of which we know contribute to an impure heart and have grave consequences (see Galatians 5:19–21). Somehow it is hard to equate envy with blatant sexual sins, but nonetheless the temptation to be envious of another person's position or blessing is still there.

The Greek word *envy* in this passage means "a feeling of resentment and jealousy toward another person because of his possessions or good qualities." James linked envy with self-seeking or selfish ambition (see James 3:14, 16). When the chief priests turned Jesus over to Pilate and asked for the release of Barabbas in His place, Pilate said they did it "because of envy" (Mark 15:10).[6]

Envy rears its ugly head at school, at the workplace, in families—even in church. It is hard to see someone move ahead of us at work or at church when we feel better qualified or have served there longer, or when we see the inheritance we think we deserve go to another family member. But we must learn to guard our hearts.

How easy it is to allow envy to move us into gossip. We quickly can pass around a rumor that is trivial, intimate or sensational—and usually only partly true—and somehow feel self-righteous or better about ourselves. To gossip about other people can have painful ramifications, bringing division and leaving deep wounds. In one of his letters, Paul warned against unrighteous men who, professing to be wise, became fools:

> Their lives became full of every kind of wickedness, sin, greed, hate, envy, murder, quarreling, deception, malicious behavior, and gossip. They are backstabbers, haters of God, insolent, proud, and boastful. . . . They know God's justice requires that those who do these things deserve to die, yet they do them anyway. Worse yet, they encourage others to do them, too.
>
> Romans 1:29–30, 32, NLT

He was writing of those who were in total rebellion against God, but isn't it interesting that along with naming the sins of hate and murder and others, he includes gossip? Note this contemporary paraphrase:

> Though some tongues just love the taste of gossip, those who follow Jesus have better uses for language than that. Don't talk dirty or silly. That kind of talk doesn't fit our style. Thanksgiving is our dialect.
>
> Ephesians 5:4, MESSAGE

While we may not set out to gossip in an effort to hurt someone, are we careful how we share in prayer groups? Do we divulge too much information when mentioning other people's problems under the guise of a prayer request?

Once I (Quin) was in a prayer meeting where the leader was giving a "praise report" for answered prayer. The group had prayed for several weeks for a woman who needed guidance because she planned to meet with her ex-husband for the first time since their divorce. But instead of simply reporting that "everything went well," the prayer leader related the detailed conversation that had taken place when the two met. I did not want to hear those intimate facts, and I never went back to that group.

"Sometimes we talk so inadvisedly," says author Lance Lambert. "Beware what you say about a message you have

> Do not let any unwholesome talk come out of your mouths, but only what is helpful for building others up according to their needs, that it may benefit those who listen. And do not grieve the Holy Spirit of God.
>
> EPHESIANS 4:29–30, NIV

heard, about someone else's testimony or their walk with the Lord, or about a work of God, even if these things are outside your present understanding."[7]

So what can we do to break this cycle of indulging in gossip? We can ask God to help us control our tongues and speak the truth in love with words that are affirming, encouraging and positive. We can determine to pray for the person being ill-spoken of and find something kind to say about him or her. When drawn into a destructive conversation about someone, we can tell those participating that we do not want to hear their report, then change the subject. If the gossip persists, we can walk away. We may lose "friends" in the process, but we will maintain a clear conscience before God.

No Prejudice Allowed

To be prejudiced toward a person or situation actually means to "prejudge" based on irrational suspicion or hatred. When we make an adverse judgment or form an opinion about a particular group, race or religion without knowledge or examination of the facts, we are expressing prejudice.[8]

Jesus called the Pharisees hypocrites for their holier-than-thou attitude that caused them to look down on others or "prejudge" them as being inferior. Jesus had compassion on all people. Most of us, if we are honest, harbor a secret prejudice of some kind. It may be as simple as not liking rich people or highly educated people, or it may involve people of a certain race or religion, or politicians, celebrities, alcoholics or even the homeless. It is important to avoid prejudice in our own lives and also guard against poisoning other people and members of our family with it.

Take Eddie, for example. He joined the Ku Klux Klan because his father was a member and Eddie considered it a family tradition. When he tried to get his wife, Linda, to embrace the Klan's ideologies, she refused. After yielding her heart to the Lord, she made six trips to a revival in Pensacola, Florida, where she kept growing in her faith. And she began praying earnestly for her husband's salvation. The answer to her prayers came when Eddie agreed to join the men of their local church on a bus trip to the revival she had been visiting.

"At that gathering, God broke prejudice off of me when I made Jesus my Lord," her husband reported. "It was a load off my shoulders." People of the race Eddie once hated are now invited to his home, and he often ministers alongside them as well. In following the Lord over the past ten years, he has been active in jail ministry and other outreaches.

"God can take a KKK man and make him a mighty man of God," Linda told us.[9]

Tony hated policemen—cops, as he called them. He could not remember why, but since childhood he had made fun of them. One summer during college break, he was working in a restaurant when a policeman came in and began a friendly conversation. Each time the officer came in, he made an effort to say hi, and Tony began to see that policemen were normal people. Maybe he could like them—after all, he was a Christian.

Then while driving home from work late one night, Tony panicked when the driver of the car behind him tried to run him off the road. As he maneuvered his car to the shoulder to avoid a crash, he welcomed the sight of a patrol car's flashing lights in pursuit of the road-rage-obsessed driver. "A policeman saved my life last night," he told his mom the next morning. Never again did she hear Tony express prejudice against an officer of the law.

Wanda grew up thinking hers was the only church. She had been taught that if you did not embrace her church's doctrine, you could not possibly go to heaven. Then she got acquainted with her neighbor, Denise, who talked about Jesus as a personal friend. Wanda discovered that her new friend truly loved the Lord and knew far more about the Bible than she did. As their friendship grew and they discussed the Bible, Wanda began to accept Christians whose doctrine differed slightly from hers, realizing that believing Jesus died on the cross for our sins was the primary basis for Christian fellowship.

Colleen's best friend during her childhood was her first cousin, Tyler. Later, when he "came out of the closet" about his sexuality, she was one of the few members of her Christian family who would still be kind to him. When Tyler died in his late twenties she grieved deeply, but she was grateful that he had felt free to share his deepest feelings with her.

Now may be a good time to stop and ask God to reveal our prejudices and then help us deal with overcoming them. Christ admonishes us:

> Judge not, that you be not judged. For with what judgment you judge, you will be judged; and with the measure you use, it will be measured back to you. And why do you look at the

speck in your brother's eye, but do not consider the plank in your own eye?

Matthew 7:1–3

The next time we are face-to-face with a person (or people group) we have greatly disliked, we can ask God to enlarge our hearts. Then we can make the effort to reach out with a smile or words of encouragement. It will not be easy at first, but with time, it will come. As we deal with rooting out any areas of prejudice, we can rest in this promise: "Therefore repent and return, so that your sins may be wiped away, in order that times of refreshing may come from the presence of the Lord" (Acts 3:19, NASB).

Some years ago, I (Quin) learned from Bible teacher Dean Sherman that when I am going through challenging situations, I should ask:

Is this a test from God?
Is this a temptation?
Is this an attack from the devil?

Testing develops character, endurance and patience (yes, God tested the children of Israel—see Deuteronomy 8:2; Judges 3:1–2, 4). *Temptation* develops a hatred of evil. But an *attack of Satan* makes me learn to depend on the Lord and resist the attack with Scripture: "Submit therefore to God. Resist the devil and he will flee from you" (James 4:7, NASB).[10]

Whatever sin we are tempted to commit, we can lean into God's promises and daily cry out, "Lord, purify my heart!" As we yield to the purifying process, the Holy Spirit can help us avoid being deceived, which we explore in our next chapter.

PRAYER

Heavenly Father, please forgive me for the sins of the flesh and the sins of the heart that I've willingly embraced. Cleanse me and make me whole, Lord, and help me to abstain from every form of evil. Separate me from profane things until I become pure and wholly consecrated to You. Lord Jesus, may my spirit, soul and body be preserved complete and blameless until the day of Your coming. Thank You for setting me free. In Jesus' name, Amen.[11]

9

Lord, Protect Me from Deception

Jesus answered and said to them: "Take heed that no one deceives you. For many will come in My name, saying, 'I am the Christ,' and will deceive many."

Matthew 24:4–5

Instead . . . of improving the gospel, carnal wisdom pollutes it, until it becomes another gospel and not the truth of God at all. All alterations and amendments of the Lord's own Word are defilements and pollutions.

—Charles Spurgeon[1]

Talk about deception! A New York volunteer firefighter admitted to setting a blaze at a local church so that he could gain attention as a hero. The eighteen-year-old was charged with a felony for third-degree arson in connection with a fire at St. Paul's Chapel in Lewisboro, New York.[2]

The word *deception* typically brings to mind meanings like "misleading," "deceitful," "dishonest" and "making a person believe what is not true." Of course, when we hear something that is blatantly false, we tend to reject it immediately. But the form of deception Jesus and others in Scripture warn against is extremely subtle—and can be perilous—because it always contains a grain of truth. Therefore, we are more likely to consider accepting an idea couched in subtle deception. And we are more likely to make wrong behavior choices.

Eve was deceived in the garden when Satan, in the form of a serpent, raised a question regarding the clear instruction God had given. After asking his leading question, Satan then challenged her: "God knows that in the day you eat of it your eyes will be opened, and you will be like God, knowing good and evil" (Genesis 3:5). Satan maligned God's character and awakened in Eve a desire to be like the Creator, which led her to eat the forbidden fruit and convince Adam to do the same. In the Fall, both Adam and Eve showed a total lack of discernment.

The enemy has continued his deceptions from that day to the present, and as a result, we see some believers doing things that are clearly unscriptural. These days we hear almost unbelievable stories of Christians being deceived:

- A widow becomes enamored of a married man she met in her church home group. When she says she has "a word from God" that he should divorce his wife and marry her, he believes it and does exactly as she tells him.

- A young Christian, flattered by the attention of a minister, gave in to his sexual advances, feeling they would be exonerated from their sin once they got married. Ten years later, finally realizing her intense desire for a husband had caused her to be deceived, she confessed to a counselor, ended the relationship and began her journey toward forgiveness and healing.

- Members of a controversial religious sect in Florida branded themselves with 666, the symbol of the Antichrist.[3]
- Hundreds of churches are installing violent video games such as the Halo series for youngsters to play before and after their youth meetings. One twelve-year-old explained the game's allure: "It's just fun blowing people up." Some pastors consider the games a successful recruiting tool to get kids to church.[4]

Self-Deception

Think for a moment. Have you ever fallen into deception because you wanted something so badly? The enemy tries many devious ways to deceive us, and all too often he succeeds.

Take for instance one friend who confessed that she lost a substantial sum by trusting a Christian man who claimed he had an invention that was guaranteed to make lots of money. She and others in her community invested in his project, but it never materialized. He skipped town with their money, leaving a lot of folks shaken up when they realized they had been fleeced.

"I was deceived, but it was my own fault," she confessed to me (Quin). "I guess I was motivated by greed and tempted by the idea of a get-rich-quick deal. I didn't check my decision with God, and I didn't check out the man's past record. Just because he said he was a Christian businessman was no reason I should have trusted him with my hard-earned money."

A. W. Tozer wrote:

When a man is deceived by another he is deceived against his will. He is contending against an adversary and is temporarily the victim of the other's guile. . . . With the self-deceived it is quite different. He is his own enemy and is working a fraud upon himself. He wants to believe the lie and is psychologically conditioned to do so. . . . Of all forms of deception, self-deception is the most deadly, and the self-deceived are the least likely to discover the fraud.

. . . How may we remain free from self-deception? The answer sounds old-fashioned and dull but here it is: Mean what you say and never say what you do not mean, either to God or man. Think candid thoughts and act forthrightly always, whatever the consequence. To do this will bring the cross into your life and keep you dead to self and to public opinion. A guileless mind is a great treasure; it is worth any price.[5]

Safeguard against Deception

Many factors can make us vulnerable to deception, such as greed or selfish desire, pride (especially spiritual pride), unwillingness to listen to counsel or submit to authority, seeking the approval of someone we admire and have placed on a pedestal, or being taken in by someone's "dynamic teaching" without searching the Scripture for ourselves.

Our safeguard against deception is *discernment*. To discern means "to separate or distinguish between; to detect with the eyes as well as to detect with senses other than vision." During the time of Judah's exile in Babylon, God spoke this indictment against her corrupt spiritual leaders: "Her priests . . . have not distinguished between the holy and unholy, nor have they made known the difference between the unclean and the clean" (Ezekiel 22:26).

When His followers asked Jesus what would be the signs of His coming, He repeatedly warned against deception, saying, "False christs and false prophets will rise and show great signs and wonders to deceive, if possible, even the elect" (Matthew 24:24; see also verses 4, 11).

How do we become discerning believers? The apostle John provides this instruction:

> Dear friends, do not believe everyone who claims to speak by the Spirit. You must test them to see if the spirit they have comes from God. For there are many false prophets in the world. . . . If a person claiming to be a prophet acknowledges that Jesus Christ came in a real body, that person has the Spirit of God. But if someone claims to be a prophet and does not acknowledge the truth about Jesus, that person is not from God.
>
> 1 John 4:1–3, NLT

Are You Making Room for the Enemy?

Because deception is such a gray area, believers without spiritual understanding and a foundation in God's Word are very vulnerable to it.

Numbers of believers seem unaware that their homes may contain items that attract demonic activity, for example video games, toys, posters, movies or music with demonic, violent or sexual themes; occultic books and magazines; souvenirs and artifacts depicting the spirits or gods of false religions and pornographic or sensual literature. Perhaps you have collected such items in your travels or unknowingly allowed family members or visitors to bring them into your home without recognizing the danger they represent.

It is important to give attention to scriptural warnings about keeping our homes free of such things, because they give the enemy a legal right to invade our lives:

> You shall burn the carved images of their gods with fire; you shall not covet the silver or gold that is on them, nor take it

for yourselves, lest you be snared by it; for it is an abomination to the LORD your God. Nor shall you bring an abomination into your house, lest you be doomed to destruction like it. You shall utterly detest it and utterly abhor it, for it is an accursed thing.

Deuteronomy 7:25–26

When Paul preached to the occult-ridden citizens of Corinth, numbers of them embraced the Gospel of Christ. The record says, "Many also of those who had believed kept coming, confessing and disclosing their practices. And many of those who practiced magic brought their books together and began burning them in the sight of everyone" (Acts 19:18–19, NASB).

To rid your home of artifacts that represent any of Satan's counterfeit gods or promote demonic activity, you may want to consider taking these steps:

- Ask the Holy Spirit to reveal to you any objectionable items, then remove them and declare that any and all spirits associated with these objects must depart in the name of Jesus Christ, as they have no right to remain (see Luke 10:19).
- Dedicate your home to the Lord. Perhaps even anoint the doorposts of your house with oil as an outward symbol that you are committing your home to God and petitioning Him for the safety of those who dwell there.
- Pray over your family members at night and ask for their health and safety, even if you do it after they are asleep.

When it comes to your children, you can keep them from watching harmful programs on TV, playing occultic or violent video games, listening to degrading music or bringing questionable objects into your home. They are under your authority until they become legal adults, and they are subject to you while they live with you.

One mom told me (Ruthanne) how her daughter came under the influence of an older teenager she met who was involved in a New Age cult group. Louisa was mystified when Kristen, her usually obedient child, became rude and rebellious and her grades in school fell dramatically. Louisa and her prayer partner began praying about the problem. A few days later, this prayer partner called and said, "I feel you need to pray over Kristen's room and ask God to show you whether or not there are any occultic objects there."

> Satan himself transforms himself into an angel of light. Therefore it is no great thing if his ministers also transform themselves into ministers of righteousness, whose end will be according to their works.
>
> 2 Corinthians 11:14–15

Louisa was always careful about what she allowed in her home, so one day while Kristen was at school, she went into her daughter's room to take a look. "Father, please show me anything in this room that is not of You that needs to be removed," she prayed. As she stood quietly looking around, she noticed light reflecting on a shiny object in the pencil holder on the desk. It was a crystal wand with a glittery cultic image attached to the top of it, which this young man had given to Kristen.

Louisa destroyed the wand, anointed the room and prayed over it, then prayed her daughter would not detect anything was missing. Within days Kristen's grades came up, her rebellion vanished and she never noticed that the object was not there. A short time later, the young man moved to another city because his father was transferred.

Parents dealing with sudden changes in their child's attitude and behavior may want to follow Louisa's example of asking God to reveal the root of the problem. Her experience is a reminder that all of us can be more vigilant about these matters and teach our children the truth of Scripture. If we take the time to seek His direction, the Holy Spirit can protect us from the enemy's strategies against us and our families.

Biblical Examples of Deception

The Bible records numerous stories of people who fell into deception. In fact, the words *deceived, deceive, deceit* or *deceitful* are mentioned 125 times in the New King James Version.

With his mother's help, Jacob deceived his father, Isaac, into giving him the blessing that rightfully belonged to the elder brother, Esau. Then Jacob himself was deceived by his father-in-law. After Jacob had labored for seven years for the hand of Rachel, Laban tricked Jacob into marrying her older sister, Leah. Years later Jacob was deceived again when his older sons sold his youngest child, Joseph, into slavery, then led their father to believe his "favorite son" was dead (see Genesis 27:1–40; 29:20–25; 37:23–34).

King David displeased God by numbering the people, but later confessed his wrongdoing. He realized he had been deceived into believing he could rely on the strength of Israel's army rather than on God, the nation's true source of strength, and God forgave him (see 2 Samuel 24).

Another example of deception is David's son, Solomon. Before becoming king of Israel, he asked God for discernment to help him govern the people. God was pleased with Solomon's request and gave him "wisdom and very great discernment" (1 Kings 4:29, NASB). For a season, he was a man who honored God and even was given the privilege of building the Temple. But later he disobeyed by taking foreign wives who deceived him and turned his heart so that he actually worshiped false gods. Unlike his father, David, Solomon did not repent. In anger, God declared the kingdom would be taken from him (see 1 Kings 9:4–7; 11:1–11).

Solomon's life illustrates the truth of Jeremiah 17:9: "The heart is deceitful above all things, and desperately wicked; who can know it? I, the LORD, search the heart, I test the mind, even to give every man according to his ways, according to the fruit of his doings."

We can take steps to avoid being deceived by:

> They [false teachers] promise freedom, but they themselves are slaves of sin and corruption. For you are a slave to whatever controls you.
>
> 2 PETER 2:19, NLT

- Constantly renewing our minds through reading the Word and obeying it
- Praying for God's direction daily
- Repenting and seeking God's forgiveness when we go astray
- Daily asking to be refilled with the Holy Spirit
- Being accountable to spiritual leaders and other believers, and accepting godly counsel from them
- Being vigilant against temptation and deception in areas we know are points of weakness for us

A Slippery Slope

Most of us would not deliberately deny our Christian faith and walk into a path of deception. But consider how we are constantly bombarded with subtle messages that erode the biblical foundation of our faith. New Age practices, once only found in a small segment of our population, have infiltrated mainstream society. We see it in the educational system, arts and entertainment, the publishing industry, corporate and financial training programs, medical practices, as well as Christian institutions and Bible-believing churches across America.

While on the surface some of these "new" concepts may seem beneficial to one's spiritual life, the terminology can be quite misleading. As believers we learn to be careful not to participate in forms of meditation and prayer that emphasize emptying our minds of all thought in order to discover the "Christ consciousness" or "higher consciousness" within us. These traditions are firmly rooted in Eastern mysticism and pagan religions.

The focus of our meditation should be on the Word of God and the comfort and guidance it provides for the believer. When in doubt about any alternative or unusual spiritual activity, it is good to ask, "Does this practice line up with what the Bible teaches?" If not, we shun it.

These days, hugely popular television programs are a major means of propagating New Age practices that appeal to people's interest in spiritual things but have no foundation in Scripture. "Oh, but they talk about God," is a common objection when a discerning believer tries to call someone's attention to the deceptive notions being taught on such programs.

> Now the Spirit expressly says that in latter times some will depart from the faith, giving heed to deceiving spirits and doctrines of demons. . . .Guard what was committed to your trust, avoiding the profane and idle babblings and contradictions of what is falsely called knowledge—by professing it some have strayed concerning the faith.
>
> 1 Timothy 4:1; 6:20–21

"It's alarming to see how many believers are being taken in by some of these ideas," one Bible teacher told us recently. "In speaking to a Christian women's group, I mentioned the error promoted by a popular TV host through the telecast and an online course by a leading occultic author. I quickly realized I had hit a sore spot, as most of these women enjoyed watching the program. Its 'feel-good' spirituality attracts them, and they don't see the deception."

God cast Satan out of heaven because this once-exalted angel, formerly called Lucifer, attempted to elevate himself above God (see Isaiah 14:12–15; Ezekiel 28:14–16). As mentioned earlier, Satan deceived our first parents by telling them they could be like God if they ate the forbidden fruit.

Today, thousands of years later, the desire to be like God remains the driving force behind false religions. Adherents of these cults believe that man is essentially good, that God is in all things and that practicing certain forms of prayer, meditation or exercise will cause you to discover "the god within."

Ray Yungen, who has done extensive research in this area, writes:

> Man and God can only be brought together through the Cross. If the all-is-one view were true, then salvation through a Redeemer would become unnecessary and pointless. In order for the Cross to make *any* sense, there must be a separation between God's perfect nature and Man's sin nature. We know Satan has only one enemy—the Cross; he knows that without it no human being can be restored to God.
>
> . . . Satan can never thwart God's ultimate plan. And yet, today's Western society is enticed by practical mystics who deny, by their own proclamations, God's plan of eternal salvation.[6]

A longtime friend of mine (Ruthanne's) was deeply involved in an occultic lifestyle before he became a Christian. But through Bible study and receiving counsel and discipling from godly leaders, he was able to change his negative behavior patterns. In writing to me of his deep concern about "Christian Yoga" classes being offered in some evangelical churches, he said this:

Yoga is just the little cup of candied poison to get the door open to even greater deceptions. As a former occult adept, I know that Yoga, also called TM or transcendental meditation, is one of the most powerful occult tools there is, and is an almost guaranteed door to the supernatural.

... You cannot Christianize Yoga—it is at its root a form of worship to pagan gods. In fact, every Yoga pose is a "prayer" representing a different Hindu god. . . . I simply cannot grasp how people can ignore this, but that is, after all, the nature of deception.

Jesus declared, "I am the way, the truth, and the life. No one comes to the Father except through Me" (John 14:6). Salvation comes only through receiving Jesus Christ as Lord and Savior. He instructed us to pray to God—but not by emptying our minds or chanting a mantra. Rather, we are to acknowledge Him as our Father, bring our requests to Him, ask for His forgiveness, forgive our offenders, pray for protection and declare His glory (see Matthew 6:7–13).

It is through such a personal relationship with Jesus, firmly grounded in Scripture, that we can keep from losing our footing on the enemy's slippery slope.

Beware of Hasty Decisions

Deception can creep up on us almost unknowingly, as Arlette, a friend of mine (Quin's), discovered when she struggled with what she thought was an unbearable situation. She married while her husband was finishing college, then both of them became active leaders in their church. Within two and a half years, they had a daughter, a son and a tight budget that forced them to borrow money to meet living expenses.

When she learned she was pregnant again, Arlette was distraught due to the pressure of their financial problems. She felt they could not afford to have a third child. Her husband, Lavon, hesitantly suggested an abortion. "It's just another form of contraception," he reasoned. "Before a baby takes its first breath, it's just a mass of cells."

Thirty years ago when this happened, the Supreme Court had just ruled that abortion was legal, and few churches spoke out against it. So without seriously seeking their pastor's counsel or God's guidance, the couple flew to another state so Arlette could undergo the procedure. Afterward, they simply pushed down their guilt and resolved to move on with their lives. When their financial situation improved, they talked about having another baby. But Arlette had sunk into an abyss of her own private grief and just could not say yes.

> Let no one deceive you with empty words, for because of these things the wrath of God comes upon the sons of disobedience. Therefore do not be partakers with them.
>
> EPHESIANS 5:6–7

Seventeen years later, knowing she needed to get free of oppressive guilt, she finally told her prayer partner what she had done. After their intense prayer time together, Arlette embarked on the road to recovery, though her healing process took several years to complete.

"I know God has forgiven me and healed me of my grief," she told me (Quin) on the phone recently. "He has used our tragedy to help others avoid similar pain and regret and to save lives." She explained how for three years she worked as a counselor at a crisis pregnancy center, sharing with young pregnant women how deceived she had been to think abortion was the answer to her dilemma.

These days, speaking as a mother and grandmother, Arlette hopes her experiences will help other women contemplating abortion avoid the trap she fell into. "Always guard against making hasty decisions," she warns, "because you will have to deal with regrets for the rest of your life."

We have seen in this chapter the importance of depending on the Holy Spirit's guidance to help us distinguish between truth and falsehood, right and wrong. And we have discussed the importance of staying grounded in the Word of God, attentive to the Holy Spirit's leading and watchful in prayer over the areas of responsibility God has given us. If we stay close to our faithful Shepherd and allow Him to lead us, we will not be deceived and go astray. Discernment will protect us from deception. And we are more likely to keep our lives in balance, as we discuss in the next chapter.

PRAYER

Lord, I pray You will protect me from error and help me walk in obedience to Your ways. Forgive me for the times when I haven't heeded the voice of the Holy Spirit. Forgive me for the times when I have acted selfishly or hastily without searching the Scriptures or seeking spiritual counsel. Help me develop a discerning heart that is attuned to Your Spirit and centered in Your truth. Amen.

10

Lord, Help Me Find Balance

As we know Jesus better, his divine power gives us everything we need for living a godly life. He has called us to receive his own glory and goodness! And by that same mighty power, he has given us all of his rich and wonderful promises.

2 Peter 1:3–4, NLT (1996 ed.)

We see life as an integrated whole where the divine rhythm of work, rest, worship and play have been personalized to create wholeness. If you are truly sensitive to God and in tune with your own life, then you know better than anyone else how to integrate these elements into your life for maximum benefit. This takes effort, courage, and discipline, and in the case of play, a little craziness.

—Richard Exley[1]

Since all of us have limited amounts of time, energy and money, it is important to learn to use these God-given resources wisely. We need God's help to develop our personal work/rest/worship/play cycle so that we keep our spiritual and physical needs in balance.

In the Talmud—the collected wisdom of the rabbis from the first five centuries—we read, "In the world to come, each of us will be called to account for all the good things God put on earth which we refused to enjoy."[2]

Finding Harmony and Balance

Our friend Billie Baptiste has purposely developed balance in her life over the years and now speaks at seminars to share what she has learned.

Some twenty years ago, Billie felt something was missing from her life. A committed Christian, she had a husband she loved, a job she liked, a teaching role at church and three children she adored who were growing quickly into adulthood. But why did she feel as though she was not really enjoying life? That New Year's, she resolved to set aside two days to seek the Lord about how she could reorder her priorities and become a good steward of God's gifts.

"I was feeling pretty frazzled and frustrated with my life—it seemed I was always a victim to the tyranny of the urgent," she remembers. "I would set out to accomplish big goals and then, just like an amoeba, I moved to where it was hot. The things I wanted to happen weren't happening, and I felt guilty about breaking so many resolutions."

During her private retreat, Billie saw that she was looking at life as a series of tasks to be accomplished, and she prayed for wisdom about how she should be using the gift of life.

"As I thought of God being the Divine Artist and myself as His creation, I realized He wanted me to have harmony and balance in my life, reflecting joy and contentment in all areas," she said. "My effectiveness should flow from my living life according to His design. God saw my life as a work in progress under His direction, but I needed to understand how I should respond to His guidance and plan."

Like many of us, Billie spent a lot of time on seemingly urgent tasks, and little time on what she considered truly important. Her perception changed when she acknowledged that God wants these six elements to come into balance: spiritual, physical, mental, social, emotional and material. Through Bible research she formulated keys to how she could reorder her life. Her diary tells of her journey:

1. Spiritual side: the part of me that seeks to have relationship with my Creator. My whole lifeline—that which keeps me going—is my relationship with God. My life goal is to have the mind of Christ. So my first year's goal was to establish a daily Bible reading program, which I've continued through all these years.

2. Physical side: the energy and movement that fuels my activities. I determined to keep myself healthy in order to continue my ministry for the Lord. I decided to lose twenty-five pounds through a weight loss program, and I found new recipes so I could prepare more nutritious meals.

3. Mental side: the intellectual reasoning, planning and processing of my activities. I admitted I was too task-oriented and needed to discover and use my talents for God's glory. I needed to "work smarter" by not concentrating so much on details, and then pare down the paperwork.

4. Social side: the desire for communication and relationship with those around me. I had been so busy that I hadn't developed a social life, which could add joy to my world. I began inviting people into my home for meals and fellowship. I found creative ways to develop

stronger bonds within my family, especially with my children.

5. Emotional side: the way I respond to life and my circumstances. My goal now was to enjoy the gift of life. This meant learning to live in the moment God had given me, right then. I had been a planner and organizer, living in the future to the extreme. I determined to sit and watch some sunsets.

6. Material side: the impact of real or perceived material needs. I had to get control of things instead of letting them control me. After making a list of all my expenditures, I began to tailor my spending to my life goals and resist making impulse purchases. I cleaned out every area of my house to get rid of clutter and had a garage sale. Like most of us, I had too much stuff. I didn't get rid of things my kids had given me, but I organized them.

"At this point, the Lord spoke to me about the prudence of allowing His plan and His timing to prevail," Billie wrote. "I wanted to get results quickly; His wisdom was to start small and accomplish an achievable mini-goal in each of these areas. I had been allowing the ways of my culture to dictate my goals; He wanted me to seek guidance from His Word to find strategy."

> Work shall be done for six days, but the seventh is the Sabbath of rest, holy to the LORD.
>
> EXODUS 31:15

Today, as a widow, Billie enjoys driving often to the beach to watch sunsets, gardening in the yard beside her patio home and creating art projects for gifts. On Saturdays she goes to an outdoor food market, enjoying the sights and smells of freshly harvested produce. She invites guests to enjoy southern Mediterranean meals served on her best china. On Sundays after attending early church, she comes home, puts on the coffee and teaches "house church" for her children and grandchildren.

Every few years, she travels to France to visit relatives. From them she learned that relaxing over a meal for two hours provides lots of family bonding, as well as fun and fellowship. Her special verse is: "Many are the plans in a man's heart, but it is the LORD's purpose that prevails" (Proverbs 19:21, NIV). Billie wants God's purpose to prevail in her life, so each day she spends quality time in prayer to seek His direction.

In his book *The Rhythm of Life*, Richard Exley makes a valid point about finding balance:

> Our world is not a very happy place. That really shouldn't surprise us. I mean, how can we expect to be happy when we violate almost every principle of the Abundant Life? We work too long, play too fast, laugh too loud and worship too little. We are materialistic. We buy things we don't need and can't afford in order to impress people we don't even like. . . . Our only hope is to learn to love God and people instead of things.[3]

Jesus, Our Example

Jesus was a master at living in "the rhythm of life"—that delicate balance between work and rest, worship and play. He was probably a carpenter until He turned thirty, then for the next three years His "work" consisted of preaching and healing. He had intimate communication with His Father in times of solitude and acknowledged a need for rest when He withdrew from the crowds.

A good deal of Jesus' ministry was home-centered. Twenty times in the gospels, He is eating or telling a story that takes place around a meal. Obviously enjoying mealtime fellowship, He often visited the Bethany home of Martha, Mary and Lazarus. He went to a wedding, dined with Pharisees and a rich tax-gatherer and even cooked breakfast for His disciples on the seashore after His resurrection.

He did not seem to get in a hurry. For example, listening to His Father's instruction, Jesus did not rush to His friend Lazarus's grave but waited a few days before going to raise him back to life. When Jairus, the ruler of the Capernaum synagogue, begged Jesus to come lay hands on his dying daughter, He stopped on the way to minister to a woman with a blood disease. Then He continued to Jairus' home and restored the girl to life (see Mark 5:22–43).

> I know that nothing is better for them than to rejoice, and to do good in their lives, and also that every man should eat and drink and enjoy the good of all his labor—it is the gift of God.
>
> ECCLESIASTES 3:12–13

How about us? We tend to rush through life at such a pace that we often fail to realize we are being governed by things we perceive as urgent—but perhaps not truly important. While we complain about how busy or tired we are, we seldom do anything about it.

Do you have a private place, a hideaway where you can step away from the noise of your workaday life and find some quiet time with the Lord? Can you shut out the world for a while? Rest and relaxation are an antidote to stress, but most of us have to purposefully find a way to make them happen. We have heard busy moms say the only quiet place they can find is in the bathroom, but all of us need more respite than that! We need time to reflect, recharge and be joyful.

Worship the Creator

Worship of almighty God helps us focus on His magnitude and vastness, and in the process our spirits are renewed. But how we worship depends on our perception of God. Do we approach our Father with awe and adoration, or with fear and dread of His condemnation? True worshipers repent for their failures and receive God's forgiveness, then forget about themselves and concentrate on Him.

I (Quin) am often guilty of handing the Lord my "request list" rather than worshiping Him for who He is. Listening to worship music helps me center on His greatness. Reading aloud from King David's psalms provides creative words to worship Him with spontaneous praise anytime and anyplace.

If you have ever been in worship when you sensed God's intense presence and power, you were changed and recharged. It happened to me one evening in Canada. I had pushed to get there because I needed renewal after spending some months in taxing travel and extensive ministry.

On my third night attending services there, I lay on my face in the back of the church, adoring and worshiping God. Suddenly, like a bolt of lightning, He touched me. I felt His glory permeating my very being. His presence was so real I thought I would just go on to heaven right then! How glad I was that I had taken the time and trouble to seek that refreshing.

For the most part, my worship times are quiet ones. I sit listening, often with my Bible open and a notebook at hand, worshiping and seeking Him. It is probably the same for you. We do not have to see lightning or hear thunder to experience His presence. *I love You, Lord. I thank You for all You've been and done for me*, is a simple enough worship moment.

At the beginning of 2008, I (Ruthanne) felt the Lord give me these verses as my primary "text" for the New Year:

> Trust in the LORD, and do good;
> Dwell in the land, and feed on His faithfulness.

163

Delight yourself also in the LORD,
   And He shall give you the desires of your heart.
Commit your way to the LORD,
   trust also in Him,
   And He shall bring it to pass.

Psalm 37:3–5

It is a very familiar passage that now has a new depth of meaning since the Lord spoke to me through it that early January morning. My part is simply to *trust Him* with all the petitions and requests I have brought before the throne—which means not worrying about how He may choose to respond to these prayers. I can enjoy His provision and simply delight in who He is, knowing He will bring to pass that which He deems best.

When I become anxious about life's problems or sense a buildup of stress, I know it is time to go outside for a walk and meditate on these verses—or have a cup of tea on my porch while enjoying the beauty of God's creation and thanking Him for His faithfulness.

Giving: A Part of Worship

Scripture clearly teaches that giving is a significant part of worship. For many Christians, tithing is an important expression of their faith, though of course it is not a condition for salvation. Pastor Jack Hayford explains that it is "a principle of giving which God has wrapped into the very structure of creation. . . . When I *let go . . . give . . . release,* I make room for life and abundance to flow into my life according to God's order."[4]

This is God's promise to us:

"Bring all the tithes into the storehouse so there will be enough food in my Temple. If you do," says the LORD of Heaven's

164

Armies, "I will open the windows of heaven for you. I will pour out a blessing so great you won't have enough room to take it in! Try it! Put me to the test!"

Malachi 3:10, NLT

Julie, the daughter of one of my (Ruthanne's) closest prayer partners, shares her story of learning this truth. After she became a single parent while still in college, her mom and I "prayed her through" many problems. But from early childhood when she got her first allowance, Julie discovered the benefit of giving 10 percent of everything she received to her church.

"I've always trusted God to be faithful in this area, even when times were hard," she told me. "I'd get unexpected checks in the mail or discounts at the store, and I believe it's God's favor in response to my tithing."

Because of her police training, Julie got an apartment rent-free by serving as security officer for the complex where she lived. One year, after having dental work done and reaching that year's limit on her insurance, she continued having problems with the same tooth. The dentist said she needed surgery, which she could not afford for another six months. But out of concern for her health, the dentist agreed to do the surgery cost-free.

"My tithe check was always the first one I wrote on payday," Julie said. "Many times I'd look at my checkbook and wonder how I'd make it, but somehow the bills got paid even when it seemed there were more bills than money. I know you can't outgive God—we just have to trust Him to do things His own way."

Recently Julie was concerned that her dad's old car needed replacing, but she could not figure out a way to help him get a new one. He seemed more concerned with helping his two daughters, both single moms. One day Julie happened to mention that she would like a car with an automatic shift. Within 24 hours, her dad called and suggested that she go pick out a new car with automatic shift, and he would take her old car with standard shift. "I feel it's the right thing to do," he said. "I'll make all the payments."

"I was able to get the car I wanted at a better price than Dad thought was possible," she said. "I've tithed consistently for most of my life because I believe God's promises, and He has always been faithful. But I never expected a blessing like this. I rejoice every day when I walk out my door and see my paid-for-by-someone-else car!"

> Do not lay up for yourselves treasures on earth, where moth and rust destroy and where thieves break in and steal; but lay up for yourselves treasures in heaven, where neither moth nor rust destroys and where thieves do not break in and steal. For where your treasure is, there your heart will be also.
>
> Matthew 6:19–21

All of us need to seek God's guidance about how we can be wise stewards of our money in order to take proper care of our families, give offerings to ministries and charities and plan for the future. If we allow our spending to get out of control, we suddenly plunge ourselves into debt. Some have found their way out of this quagmire by writing down their out-of-pocket expenses to discover some of their spending weaknesses. Then they stopped buying on impulse.

For instance, I (Quin) have a friend who had an obsession with shoes. Once she went into a store and bought a beautiful pair of multicolored leather shoes she had admired in the window—even though they were two sizes too small. "I can only wear these shoes for two hours without them hurting me, but I've just got to have them," she told me. Today, ten years later, after she resolved to limit her spending in every area of her life, she has a small rack of shoes in her small house. And she uses her "extra money" to support ministries in the Middle East.

Following my friend's example will help us make better choices in spending our resources and keep us from going into debt.

Stress Knocks Us Off-Balance

The human body's instinct to defend itself when it senses a threat of some sort produces stress. This can be a good thing in emergencies, because it causes us to jump out of the way of an oncoming car or shield a child who is in harm's way. But if stress is prolonged, it can cause health problems.

Changes in our routine can make us feel stressed—and of course several changes coming all at once only increase the pressure. Some common sources of stress are losing a job, moving, money problems, caring for elderly parents or an ill family member, death of a spouse, an injury or illness, a divorce or marriage, having a baby or having your child leave or return home. Here are suggestions for dealing with stress:

- Pray and ask God for direction and strategies to help you.
- Determine not to worry about things you cannot control, such as the weather, traffic jams or other people's decisions.
- Prepare to the best of your ability for events you know may be stressful, then ask God for His peace.
- Try to look at change as a positive challenge, not as a threat.
- Work to resolve conflicts with other people.
- Talk to a trusted friend, family member or counselor about your challenge.
- Set realistic goals at home and at work.

- Exercise on a regular basis.
- Eat well-balanced meals and get enough sleep.
- Take time for activities that you do not find stressful, such as social events, sports or hobbies.[5]

> Be careful how you live. Don't live like fools, but like those who are wise. Make the most of every opportunity in these evil days. Don't act thoughtlessly, but understand what the Lord wants you to do.
>
> EPHESIANS 5:15–17, NLT

With God's help, we can restore our spiritual and emotional energies—finding a lifestyle that will replenish our inner man. He wants us to achieve balance in our lives to maintain good spiritual, physical, mental and emotional health.

We Need to Work

Since work is a necessary part of life, God wants us to do it with diligence, integrity and pride while enjoying the fruit of our labor. Paul admonishes that "whatever you do in word or deed, do all in the name of the Lord Jesus, giving thanks to God the Father through Him" (Colossians 3:17). This puts work in a whole new perspective.

Work provides food on our table and a roof over our heads—it keeps us going. But when work becomes the all-consuming passion of a man or woman, it is idolatry. Sadly, far too many people have become workaholics, driven to success by their own ambition. Wrapped up in what they do, they display a blind devotion to work.

If you wonder whether or not you are a workaholic, answer these questions: Do you overschedule yourself? Multitask most of the time? Neglect personal needs such as sleep, recreation and food? Value your job over your family? Have little time for Bible reading, prayer and maintaining relationships?

Workaholics tend to equate their identity with their jobs, and they unconsciously use work and busyness to avoid intimacy. But living a balanced life enhances our overall well-being. Maybe you know someone like these folks who are addicted to work:

- Dick is so busy at the office that he has never seen his son play soccer. He just cannot pull himself away from work.
- Martha brings her work home and cannot put it down long enough to have fun with her husband, even to attend his company picnic.
- Paul is a pastor who seems to spend more time with his flock than with his own children. Emergency calls from members of his congregation rate higher than his family's needs.
- Frances is a sales rep who makes good money, travels a lot and leaves her teenagers and husband to fend for themselves. She is never around for her children's special activities.
- Brett will attend certain family and social events, but instead of interacting with those present, he takes incoming calls on his cell phone or spends much of the time text-messaging his work colleagues.

Take Time for Leisure

People involved in ministry are just as susceptible to the workaholic syndrome as those in the business world. Regardless of our occupation, we can easily get so caught up in daily responsibilities and activities that we seldom think about taking time for relaxation, reflection and leisure. Our friend Rose, a minister's wife, wrote us about how she and her husband, Bobby, have learned the importance of resisting this tendency. She shares in her own words:

No matter where you live or work, it's easy to overdo and work too much, and for a person with many abilities, it's even harder to say no. Bobby and I are now in a position where the leadership of our church requires staff members to try to maintain balance in their lives and keep their families as their first priority. Since most of us really don't know how to do this, it takes work and changing old thought patterns.

About three years ago, Bobby and I started doing what we call a "vision retreat," with the two of us staying at a hotel for a couple of days to be alone. It was awkward at first to focus on ourselves, but our relationship began changing and growing as we sowed time and energy into each other in a more deliberate way. We talked about our relationship, our son and daughter, our dreams for the future, our mistakes in the past and our relationship with God.

> Now may the God of peace who brought up our Lord Jesus from the dead . . . make you complete in every good work to do His will, working in you what is well pleasing in His sight.
>
> HEBREWS 13:20–21

We now schedule time for this at least twice a year. We have always loved each other, but now our love and enjoyment of one another is greater than either of us imagined it could be. We enjoy taking long drives, eating pizza and watching DVDs, just being together. Last year a friend let us stay at a condo in Colorado for five days for our thirtieth anniversary. We shared our hearts with each other and laughed and cried as we were refreshed and strengthened.

Of course, every time we do this we take the risk of being vulnerable, but trust in one another is very important. We've not always had this trust, so I don't want anyone to think it has been easy to get to this place. God has done much healing in our relationship over the years as we've been willing to forgive one another for mistakes both of us have made.

When our son got married in Australia, we did a "vision retreat" as a family. We stayed at a beach house for four days, and each day we shared, one couple at a time, about our hopes and dreams for the future and our hurts and pains of the past and present. We had a time of repentance and forgiveness and prayed for each other. It was one of the most awesome times of our lives. We also had fun shopping, playing golf, watching kangaroos, walking the beach and visiting Hillsong Church.

Life is not perfect for any of us—we all struggle and have to work hard at being all God has created us to be. But we're grateful for His blessing on the seeds Bobby and I have sown into each other's lives. The law of sowing and reaping works in relationships, on both the positive and negative sides, but I believe God makes up for our losses and mistakes.

In his book *When I Relax I Feel Guilty*, Tim Hansel says:

> More today than ever, we need to learn how to give ourselves permission to relax, to play, to enjoy life, and to enjoy God for who He is. We play in order to work better or to be more useful to God.
>
> . . . Do you take time to play? Do you know how to play? Do you have time to rest? Do you even know what it means? Interestingly enough, Scripture not only calls us to enter into God's rest, but to live out of that rest. The temptation to overwork is potentially one of the greatest problems for dedicated, sincere Christians today.[6]

While we do have limited amounts of time and energy, God can help us balance our work/rest/worship/play cycle. This not only gives us more joy in life, it makes us more useful to His Kingdom. And it will help us to stay free from the bondage of the bad habits we have managed to overcome, which we will discuss next, in our final chapter.

PRAYER

Lord, I need Your help to get my life in balance. I want to live life to the fullest, as You intended, and I also want to glorify You in all I do. Please show me the areas where I need to change. Then help me be willing and give me strength to follow through. Thank You for Your guidance and Your love for me. In Jesus' name, Amen.

11

Staying Free

Stand fast therefore in the liberty by which Christ has made us free, and do not be entangled again with a yoke of bondage.

Galatians 5:1

There are no second-class citizens in the Kingdom of God. We are fellow citizens in His household. Let Him heal your wounds, forgive your sins, dispel your fears, sort out your confusions, and reveal to you the glory that you *are* in Him. Once that reality has been established in your heart, no one will be able to take it from you.

—Paula Sandford[1]

As we have seen throughout this book, we are all creatures of habit. And the habits we acquire affect who we become. It is the undesirable habits we want to put a stop to—complaining, worrying, being fearful, manipulating, eating compulsively, smoking, drinking and others.

With strategy and persistence, we can break our bad habits just as surely as we formed them. "Habit is overcome by habit," wrote Thomas á Kempis, a fifteenth-century German monk. His observation is still true today. The key is consistency and dependence on God's help. Here are some suggestions:

- Recognize, admit and desire to overcome the problem, whether it is negative self-talk, anger, envy, criticism, unhealthy eating or whatever your weak area may be. The key is to start with one bad habit and work to overcome it, then take on the next-most-annoying habit you need to break.

- Decide on a plan of action. Consciously choose to replace the bad habit with a practice that is good for you. If you are a negative thinker, for instance, replace a pessimistic thought with a positive one, even by memorizing Scripture or writing down your blessings.

- Choose to get your body in shape. Establishing an exercise routine and eating more nutritious food can help you gain a healthier body, feel better about yourself and possibly increase your energy in the process.

- Find a creative replacement. For every bad habit you kick, find a creative way to use your time, energy and God-given talents constructively. For instance, one man replaced his compulsive card-playing habit with doing something he really enjoyed—using his woodworking tools to build things with his kids.

A Spirit of Gratitude

When we come clean with the Lord about our need to change, He is more than willing to reveal hidden issues in our hearts that have ensnared us and hindered our freedom. Giving heed to this Scripture is good advice: "Be self-controlled and alert. Your enemy the devil prowls around like a roaring lion looking for someone to devour. Resist him, standing firm in the faith" (1 Peter 5:8–9, NIV). We need to continually guard against allowing the enemy to pull us back into doing those things we hate.

Joenett is a military wife who shared with me (Quin) how she and her family were able to stop the ungrateful habit of complaining. When the Air Force transferred her husband to northwest Florida, there was no housing on base for their family of three. They stayed in one room for a month, then got housing at a nearby base. The two bedrooms with one bath was a big change from their four-bedroom, two-bath home in North Carolina.

"We were complaining about everything from the crowded house to the lack of shopping outlets as we compared almost everything unfavorably with the city we'd left behind," Joenett reported. "One day the Lord reminded me that because of their complaining, the children of Israel died in the wilderness and never reached the Promised Land. I said, 'Lord, I don't want to die in Florida—help me get over this bad habit.'"

> Search me, O God, and know my heart;
> Try me, and know my anxieties;
> And see if there is any wicked way in me,
> And lead me in the way everlasting.
>
> Psalm 139:23–24

She labeled a Styrofoam cup with the words "Complaining Cup" and placed it on the kitchen counter. She and her husband and six-year-old daughter agreed that whenever one of them complained, they had to put one dollar in the cup. She recorded the complaints, and at the end of the week whoever had complained the least would get the money in the cup.

"My husband, with his quiet personality, always seemed to get the money," she said. "My daughter got tired of losing her allowance just because she complained. After a month or so, we were complaining less and less. Instead, we were thanking the Lord every night for the roof over our heads, for our bathroom, for unusual places to explore we had not considered and that my husband was with us and not stationed overseas.

"As our blessing list grew, we developed a new motto: *Try new things without complaining*. At last our bad habit was broken."

Standing on God's Word

Countless numbers of parents have agonized in prayer when they have seen their children become bound by addictive behavior. Marilou knew tragedy lay ahead for her son Blake when casual drinking in high school led to his becoming an alcoholic. For fifteen years, she prayed for him because he seemed bent on self-destruction. He would go for long spells of normalcy when he was sober, working and attending church. Then he would go on a drinking binge, displaying erratic behavior.

Family members often asked, "How can you stand it? Aren't you going out there to try to rescue him?"

"No, not until the Lord tells me to," Marilou would reply. "I'm standing firm in prayer and on God's promises." And pray she did, even taking her praying friends with her to intercede and worship God in Blake's bedroom wherever he lived.

Once when he passed out at her house, Marilou sat beside him, praying and weeping as God allowed her to feel some of his pain. Another time, when Blake drank some mouthwash in his desperation for alcohol, she cried out to God to keep her son safe. His deer-hunting rifles were in a nearby closet, and she feared he might harm himself.

One night Marilou went to a gospel sing, very distraught because Blake had just wrecked his car. When a trio sang and one of the men in the group gave his testimony of getting free from alcohol, she listened closely. "As he quoted a Scripture, I felt the words flew through the air and landed right in my heart," she said.

This was the verse: "He who has begun a good work in you will complete it until the day of Jesus Christ" (Philippians 1:6). The Lord said to Marilou, *That's for your son.*

For two more very rough years, Marilou clung to that word from God with renewed hope. When discouragement hit, she would receive something in the mail such as a calendar or bookmark with her Scripture promise on it. During that time, God carried her in what she calls "a walk of faith."

> But now you are free from sin and have become slaves of God. This brings you a life that is only for God, and this gives you life forever. The payment for sin is death. But God gives us the free gift of life forever in Christ Jesus our Lord.
>
> ROMANS 6:22–23, NCV

Blake moved to California, where he planned to go to sea with the Merchant Marines, but he was rejected because of a bad report on his heart. Illness and another round of drinking finally made him desperate enough to call his parents. "Dad, I've got to come home," he pleaded. "I can't make it. I'm at the bottom."

That same day, Marilou's husband flew to California and brought their son home. Soon after arriving, Blake had a seizure and felt God was telling him, *Choose life or choose death.* In his heart Blake wanted life, but he did not realize how hard that choice would be.

After going on another drinking binge, he ended up in an apartment strewn with broken glass, with the unlit gas stove on. His parents decided to use a law in their state that allowed them to have their adult son committed to a treatment facility. Not realizing they did it out of love and concern for him,

Blake was so angry he would not even speak to his parents for some time. But he completed the program, got further help after his release and never took another drink after that.

Blake married, became a father and enrolled in seminary. Today, at forty-two, he has been alcohol-free for six years and has thanked his parents many times for committing him to a treatment center. Blake recently became senior pastor of a church and is finishing his master's degree in seminary.

Can a mother's faithful prayers pay off? Marilou assures us they do. And she is grateful that God helped her to stand in faith instead of giving in to despair.

Steps to Breaking Addictions

Of course, twelve-step treatment programs do help many addicts, but most of them acknowledge that human resolve alone seldom brings about long-term change. Author and psychiatrist Dr. John White wrote that the most effective results come through a program that emphasizes honestly confronting the problem, while developing a personal relationship with Christ. He suggests the following ten steps as a Christian-based plan:

1. I face the fact and tell God I now know that I am helpless. I tell Him I need to see clearly.
2. I tell God I need to see my own inner nature as well as His greatness and kindness. I accept His promise to show me all I need to see.
3. I offer my body as a living sacrifice to God, and as an act of worship.
4. In repentance I ask God to search my heart by praying Psalm 139:23–24. I promise God: "As You do so, I will write down those sins and failures to which You draw my attention."

5. God helping me, I will admit to myself, to God and also to a friend the exact nature of my sins. Lord, please give me a friend to whom I may be accountable.

6. Lord, I want to be entirely ready for You to remove every sinful tendency in me. So far as I know, I am ready. But go on testing me, showing me where my motives are phony.

7. I know You are willing to forgive me, but I ask You to make Your forgiveness clear in the deepest parts of my being and not just in my intellect. Show me I am forgiven indeed. Show me the love of Christ as shown on the cross.

8. I will make a list of people I have hurt and wronged, beginning with those closest to me. I face before God my responsibility to act.

9. Wherever I can, I will make amends, and do so as soon as possible.

10. God, I resolve to come before You at certain special times in the future to allow You to examine my heart and life.[2]

Bearing Fruit

Years ago, beside Mobile Bay on the coast of Alabama, I (Quin) passed a small fenced-in area that was piled high with trash and junk. "Look at the bad habits we picked up," a sign over the spot explained. Words I had heard in a sermon a few days earlier came back to me: "God can take the garbage and make a compost heap to fertilize the fruit in our lives."

Perhaps the most effective way we can avoid the pitfalls of bad habits and bad attitudes is to cultivate these fruits of the Holy Spirit in our lives: love, joy, peace, patience, kindness, goodness, faithfulness, gentleness and self-control (see Galatians 5:22–23).

To do this, we first must acknowledge that only the Holy Spirit working through us can produce fruit. Left to our own devices, we tend to produce weeds, thorns and thistles. Next, we need to realize that cultivating fruit is not an event, but a process. Receiving Christ as our Savior occurs the moment we acknowledge Him as Lord and receive His forgiveness from sin. But becoming a mature, fruit-bearing believer takes place over time as we resist doing things our own way and yield to the ways of the Holy Spirit.

One friend shared how she determined to call on the Lord for help when her patience was tested or stress threatened to overwhelm her. Instead of dealing with these frustrations in her usual way, she would stop and consciously yield her will to God in every difficult circumstance. It became her habit to pray, "Lord, You've got to work in this situation—in how I respond, what I say, what I do." As this became a way of life for her, her example inspired others to allow the Holy Spirit to develop these Christlike traits in them as well. Jesus gives us the key to achieving this goal:

> Abide in Me, and I in you. As the branch cannot bear fruit of itself, unless it abides in the vine, neither can you, unless you abide in Me. I am the vine, you are the branches. He who abides in Me, and I in him, bears much fruit; for without Me you can do nothing.
>
> John 15:4–5

Forgiving an Ex-Husband

As we discussed in chapter 5, unforgiveness has a way of lying hidden and dormant in our hearts so we are not even aware of it. One painful experience from the past, not confronted and dealt with, can keep us from enjoying the present. Our next story illustrates how one extremely hurtful incident robbed a friend of her enjoyment of life for far too long.

Doris hated Christmas. For seventeen miserable years, a melancholy cloud hung over her during the holiday season. The reason—after only three years of marriage, her husband had chosen Christmastime to announce he was leaving her for another woman. Her self-esteem plummeted. Year after year, she barely made it through gift buying for family and friends, while avoiding office parties and neighborhood get-togethers. She would not even listen to Christmas music because painful memories controlled her.

Then she made a decision and took action. "Devil, you aren't going to rob me of any more Christmases!" she shouted one day. Doris had already told the Lord many times that she forgave her ex-husband. But in the recesses of her heart, she still clung to shreds of bitterness over what he had done. When she planned a trip to her hometown to visit her family, she asked her brother to arrange a face-to-face meeting with her ex-husband.

He was now married with a family of his own, so of course she could not go back into that relationship. But she wanted to tell him face-to-face that she forgave him, so she could move forward into her own future with confidence. They had a friendly visit in which they said to one another, "I forgive you." He even gave her a hug and apologized for handling their divorce the way he had. She left with her self-esteem once again intact.

"I had been in emotional bondage to him all those years over feeling abandoned," Doris told me (Quin). "I couldn't restore the marriage, but I needed to have closure. The key was choosing to forgive and not allowing the devil to rob me of any more holiday seasons."

When she began enjoying listening to Christmas carols again and cheerfully dropped money into the Salvation Army kettles, Doris knew she was back in the Christmas spirit.

Let's review the steps Doris finally took to get free from her hurts, disappointments and insecurities:

- She went from denial to admitting that she needed to address her problem and forgive her ex-husband once and for all.
- She took action. Though she thought she had forgiven him in a general way, she had to address specific issues involved—primarily her sense of abandonment. Talking to him in person helped accelerate her healing.
- She accepted herself and determined to look at Christmas with a positive attitude. The enemy was no longer able to torment her thoughts, rob her self-esteem or steal her joy during the holidays.

As Doris discovered, even one traumatic experience can have a strong negative impact on a person's sense of well-being. When a series of such incidents occur, the cumulative effect becomes even more damaging, as we see in our next story.

Staying Free from PTSD

Post-traumatic stress disorder (PTSD) is a psychological condition people may experience following domestic violence, severe accidents, sexual assault, natural disasters, terrorist attacks, war experiences and a host of other incidents. Given the violent atmosphere of today's world, the number of people affected by this problem is increasing.

While working as a school counselor, our friend Joyce often had to deal with such traumas in the lives of her students. At the same time, she was coping with traumatic events in her own family. She shares her story in her own words:

Seven years ago, I attended a conference for training on how to handle trauma in our schools, such as shootings, gang fights, suicide and other disasters, and how to deal with PTSD in the aftermath of such events. That trip turned out to be the beginning of my own yearlong journey of healing from this disorder.

For some time I had often felt insecure at home and in public places—edgy and "on alert" for no apparent reason. I had trouble sleeping and was constantly looking for a place of safety. In a restaurant, I'd want to know where the exits were. If I was in a large room with furniture, I'd imagine finding a place to hide under a table or under the leaves of a big plant. As the conference speaker described various reactions students may have to trauma, I realized he was describing the very symptoms I was experiencing.

Over the previous two years, I had become a single mom responsible for two preteens. We survived two attempted break-ins and a drive-by shooting in which a single bullet shattered our glass storm door (all of which happened at night). With the first break-in attempt, I was on the phone with the 9-1-1 operator while the robbers were on the other side of the patio door trying to break in, but when I pounded on the glass they ran away. Neither the robbers nor the drive-by shooter were caught,

> He has sent Me to heal the brokenhearted,
> To proclaim liberty to the captives,
> And the opening of the prison to those who are bound . . .
> To comfort all who mourn,
> To console those who mourn in Zion,
> To give them beauty for ashes,
> The oil of joy for mourning,
> The garment of praise for the spirit of heaviness.
>
> Isaiah 61:1–3

though police reports were filed. Later, my younger daughter was sexually abused by a youth minister of our church.

At the seminar, I realized that all these events compounded together led to my experiencing PTSD. With a mixture of relief and anxiety, I admitted to the counselor friend who was with me that I was suffering from most of these symptoms. Up until now I had not discussed this with anyone. I had told the Lord that I chose to forgive the people responsible for these traumas, and occasionally I would make declarations accordingly during my prayer time. Yet I failed to see in myself the indicators of PTSD behavior.

I had been seeing a counselor, more to learn new skills for my own practice than for any other reason. But I called him every day during the four-day conference for advice on what to do. One recovery therapy is physical exercise, so he told me to climb stairs two or three times a day at the conference hotel. As the speaker gave ideas for treating PTSD, I would put them into practice.

After the conference, I took an already-scheduled vacation trip to visit Annie, a special Christian friend in Canada who is a dance therapist. I am also a dancer, so I was eager to share experiences with her. But God had a bigger plan. I explained to Annie what had happened the week before, and she willingly helped me on the healing journey. I danced, worked with clay and paint and had experiential time with her as I worked through the emotions of the traumas I'd experienced.

With PTSD victims, talking by itself usually is not enough; the feelings must be expressed outwardly. For me, movement was a natural medium of expression. And of course Annie and I shared many times of prayer. These were important steps in the process of achieving my freedom:

- Admitting that I was a victim of trauma and PTSD
- Deciding I was not going to live as a victim

- Taking advantage of the help God provided
- Refusing to identify with the trauma—instead identifying who I am in Christ and how He created me
- Renewing my mind through prayer and Scripture reading
- Eating right and exercising
- Massive journaling
- Sacred dancing

I was set free from PTSD, yet I had to take precautions to prevent a relapse. Praying with others and praying to stay in communion with God were essential. When I felt myself getting into the old fear-anxiety pattern, I would call one of three particular friends who were always available to pray with me. Doing intensive experiential therapy as I needed it was also invaluable.

The greatest challenge for me was reining in my thoughts and emotions, which required great discipline. For example, when I would hear the sound of breaking glass, instead of tensing, I had to immediately repeat my mainstay Bible verses. Having the Word in my spirit and available at those times would chase the other thoughts away.

The verses I held to were all of Psalm 91, plus these: "The name of the LORD is a strong tower; the righteous run to it and are safe" (Proverbs 18:10). "Hold me up, and I shall be safe" (Psalm 119:117). "Whoever listens to me will dwell safely, and will be secure, without fear of evil" (Proverbs 1:33).

I kept a Bible in the car, on my desk, on my dining room table and by my bed. At first, when frightening thoughts would bombard my mind, I literally would run to get a Bible. I have now remained free of PTSD symptoms for more than seven years, gloriously healed.

Because harboring bitter feelings can have such damaging effects, we want to share one more story about the importance of letting go of wounds from the past. In this case, the issue gravely affected a friend's physical health until God revealed to her the source of the problem.

What's Eating You?

Breast cancer! The diagnosis is scary, the outcome uncertain. But Clara and her husband faced it together in prayer.

"When we got the diagnosis, we prayed for God's more excellent way," she says. "We agreed to have the doctor remove only the suspicious lump and gave him explicit instructions not to perform a mastectomy."

After the surgery, when tests showed cancer cells were still present, the doctor did recommend a mastectomy. But Clara again refused, believing God's plan for her did not include radical surgery, radiation or chemotherapy. Then she plunged into an intense Bible study regarding issues of the heart.

"What am I eating that is wrong?" she asked the Lord one day during her prayer time.

It's what's eating you—not what you are eating, the Lord admonished her. Bowing her head in repentance, Clara confessed that she did have issues—people to forgive, attitudes to adjust, offenses to give up. She and her husband were pastors, and she had walked with the Lord many years. Although she thought she had a "clean slate," she admitted that hurts from the past were festering deep within her. After a time of asking God's forgiveness for things she remembered, Clara and her husband agreed on a strategy to help her move toward wholeness. It included:

- Changing her diet—making sure her eating habits were healthful.
- Taking Holy Communion together every day.
- Confessing, both to the Lord and to her husband, any faults God revealed to her.
- Praying continually for cancer cells to leave her body.
- Making biblical declarations daily concerning her complete healing.

A year later, Clara got an "all clear" report—the doctor found no cancer cells in her breast. She still takes Communion every day and declares God's health promises from Scripture. And based on her studies, she is ready to write a book on heart issues. Clara says her freedom came as a process over time, but that she sees the need for vigilance to maintain this freedom.

By relating Clara's story, we are not advocating that anyone go against doctor's recommendations regarding medical treatment—this is a personal matter for each individual to decide. We are just reporting what one woman's walk to freedom involved.

> Indeed, we had the sentence of death within ourselves so that we would not trust in ourselves, but in God who raises the dead; who delivered us from so great a peril of death, and will deliver us, He on whom we have set our hope. And He will yet deliver us.
>
> 2 CORINTHIANS 1:9–10, NASB

Maybe you, like Clara, want to ask yourself these questions to help maintain your freedom from bad habits that once beset you: Do I refuse to let go of old hurts and wounds? . . . to forgive others for what they did? . . . to stop judging others? . . . to allow God to change my heart? . . . to confess my sins to someone I can trust? In other words, am I making excuses for my "household sins"? Dealing with such things in your life can make all the difference in becoming spiritually, mentally, emotionally and physically whole.

Finding Freedom with God's Help

As we have seen throughout this book, those who experienced true freedom from their bad habits usually took steps afterward to guard their victory. Others changed their way of thinking. Many asked God to intervene in their weakest areas, enabling them to become strong. Still others have only begun their journey to staying free, but they are well on the way.

At the start, we explored why we do the things we hate and how our human resolve will not be enough to change us—we need to trust God for His help. We saw how important it is to know that God loves and accepts us and wants to help us change. And He will!

Sometimes our habitual ways of reacting to life's challenges show that we need to respond differently, which is why we talked about the importance of developing self-control, staying calm in a crisis and avoiding fear and worry. We also covered how to handle grief when we face disappointment or loss. All of us face such heartbreaks at some time in our lives, and grieving in a healthy way is essential so we can heal and continue to walk in the freedom God intends for us.

In many cases our bad habits are "household sins," plain and simple—poor behavioral patterns we have become comfortable with, which we are reluctant to surrender. Those habits certainly need changing. We also looked at the consequences of holding on to unforgiveness. Refusing to forgive others is a devastating habit, but when we let go of bitterness, amazing blessings result from obeying God in this area. The greatest blessing in forgiving others is knowing our heavenly Father will then forgive us.

We examined many kinds of addictions that can become both idols and entrapments of the enemy. We saw that sheer willpower on our part does not suffice in breaking addictions.

But when we turn to God and ask for His intervention, He always does His part to help us find freedom.

We also discussed manipulative behavior, contrasting it with the peace available in laying down our tendency to control others or to be controlled. Then we discovered the good fruit of keeping a pure heart.

We talked about how we can safeguard ourselves from deception by praying for and employing discernment. And very importantly, we saw that we can avoid forming bad habits in the first place by determining to live balanced lives in every area, whether at work, rest, worship or play.

Though we are all creatures of habit, we can take positive steps toward breaking our bad habits and replacing them with healthy routines instead. So we end where we began: Like the apostle Paul, we, too, long to stop doing the things we hate.

With God's help and our cooperation, we can!

PRAYER

Father, thank You that Jesus shed His blood on the cross and provided a way for my sins to be covered. I accept Jesus' sacrifice for me and receive Your forgiveness and cleansing. Lord, help me to yield my will to You in every area, allowing the Holy Spirit to work deeply in my heart. I want to continually abide in You, bear the fruit of the Holy Spirit in my life and walk in complete freedom. Amen.

Notes

Introduction

1. *Webster's New Explorer Dictionary and Thesaurus*, s.v. "habit."

Chapter 1: Why Do I Do the Things I Hate?

1. Neil Anderson, *Victory Over the Darkness: Realizing the Power of Your Identity in Christ* (Ventura, Calif.: Regal, 2000), 81.

2. "Tennessee Mother Makes Daughter Stand on Street Corner Wearing Sign Listing Bad Behavior," *Associated Press*, June 25, 2007, http://www.foxnews.com.

3. Adapted from Kathe Wunnenberg, *Grieving the Child I Never Knew* (Grand Rapids: Zondervan, 2001), 93–95.

4. David Augsburger, *Caring Enough to Confront* (Ventura, Calif.: Gospel Light, 1981).

5. "Church Challenge: Curbing Criticism," *Daily News* (Fort Walton Beach, Fla.), October 21, 2006.

6. Oswald Chambers, *My Utmost for His Highest*, updated ed. (Grand Rapids: Discovery House, 1992), August 28 entry (readings by date).

Chapter 2: Lord, I Need to Know You Accept Me

1. See http://www.quotegarden.com/god.html, third quote listed.

2. Adapted from seminar material by Pia Mellody, RN, CSAC. Her material is available at http://www.piamellody.com.

3. Dr. Diane Langberg, *Feeling Good, Feeling Bad* (Ann Arbor: Servant, 1991), 52–54.

4. Ibid.

5. James Strong, *Strong's Exhaustive Concordance*, Biblesoft's *PC Bible Study*, 2007. Greek reference #4161.

6. Adapted from Dr. Mark Johnson, *Spiritual Warfare for the Wounded* (Ann Arbor: Servant, 1992), 90.

Chapter 3: Lord, Help Me Stay Calm

1. Jamie Buckingham, *Coping with Criticism* (Plainfield, N.J.: Logos International, 1978), 88.

2. Read more about Gail McWilliams's story at http://www.gailmcwilliams. com.

3. Elisabeth Elliot, *Keep a Quiet Heart* (New York: Walker and Company, 1998), 104, 106.

4. The National Women's Health Resource Center, U.S. Department of Health and Human Services, http://www.healthywomen.org (search for "caregivers"), or call 1-877-986-9472.

Chapter 4: Lord, Take Away My Worry, Fear and Grief

1. Hannah Whitall Smith, *The God of All Comfort* (Chicago: Moody, 1956), 112.

2. Corrie ten Boom, *Clippings from My Notebook* (Nashville: Thomas Nelson, 1982), 33.

3. Jack W. Hayford, ed., *Spirit-Filled Life Bible* (Nashville: Thomas Nelson, 1991), 1415.

4. Fred Smith, "Wait to Worry," *The Christian Reader*, published by *Christianity Today*, June 1993, 53.

5. Catherine Marshall, *Something More* (Carmel, N.Y.: *Guideposts* Associates ed., 1974), 62–63.

6. Ibid., 63.

7. Ibid., 67–68.

8. Barbara Johnson, *Pack Up Your Gloomies in a Great Big Box, Then Sit on the Lid and Laugh!* (Dallas: Word, 1993), 32.

9. Ruth Sissom, *Instantly a Widow* (Grand Rapids: Discovery House, 1990), 20.

Chapter 5: Lord, Enable Me to Forgive

1. Jack Hayford, *The Key to Everything* (Lake Mary, Fla.: Creation House, 1993), 40.

2. *Merriam Webster Online Dictionary*, s.v. "forgive." See also James Strong, *Strong's Exhaustive Concordance*, Biblesoft's *PC Bible Study*, 2007. Greek references on "forgive," #630, #863, #5483.

3. "Killer's Wife Salutes Amish Mercy," *Sky News*, October 4, 2006, http://www.foxnews.com.

4. See http://blip.tv/file/815590.

Chapter 6: Lord, I Can't Stop Myself

1. Archibald D. Hart, *Healing Life's Hidden Addictions* (Ann Arbor: Servant, 1990), 19.

2. Erwin W. Lutzer, *Getting to NO: How to Break a Stubborn Habit* (Charlotte: Billy Graham Evangelistic Association, with permission from David C. Cook, 2007), 33.

3. "Health and Fitness News," *Frontlines* newsletter, Christian Broadcasting Network, August 2004, 4.

4. Mark Rutland, *Character Matters* (Lake Mary, Fla.: Charisma, 2003), 98.

5. Dr. Martin Wasserman, quoted in "Video Game Overuse May Be an Addiction," *HealthDay News*, June 22, 2007, http://www.forbes.com.

6. Ibid.

Chapter 7: Lord, Help Me Stop Taking Control

1. Deborah Smith Pegues, *Thirty Days to Taming Your Tongue* (Eugene, Ore.: Harvest House, 2005), 23.

2. Elisabeth Elliot, *Keep a Quiet Heart* (New York: Walker and Company, 1998), 52–53.

3. Elizabeth Barrett Browning biography in "Sermon Illustrations," taken from *Daily Walk*, May 30, 1992, http://net.bible.org, and Browning's *Sonnet 43*.

4. Hayford, *Spirit-Filled Life Bible*, 1694.

Chapter 8: Lord, Purify My Heart

1. Alice Smith, *Delivering the Captives* (Minneapolis: Bethany, 2006), 22.

2. From *Christianity Today's* online *Leadership Journal*, March 2005, http://www.blazinggrace.org/pornstatistics.

3. Mike Genung, "Statistics and Information on Pornography in the USA," http://www.blazinggrace.org.

4. Ted Roberts, *Pure Desire* (Ventura, Calif.: Regal, 1999), 26, 74–75.

5. Judy Reamer, *Feelings Women Rarely Share* (Springdale, Penn.: Whitaker, 1987), 51.

6. *Nelson's Illustrated Bible Dictionary*, © 1986, Thomas Nelson Publishers, PC Study Bible software.

7. Lance Lambert, *Experiencing Spiritual Protection* (West Sussex, England: Sovereign World Limited, 1991), 47.

8. *American Heritage Dictionary of the English Language*, 4th ed. (Boston: Houghton Mifflin, 2003), s.v. "prejudice."

9. See more of Linda and Eddie's story in Quin Sherrer and Ruthanne Garlock, *Lord, I Need to Pray with Power* (Lake Mary, Fla.: Charisma, 2007), 129–30.

10. From my (Quin's) lecture notes taken during a Dean Sherman presentation, and from his book *Spiritual Warfare for Every Christian* (Seattle: Frontline Communications, 1990).

11. Prayer based on 1 Thessalonians 5:22–23.

Chapter 9: Lord, Protect Me from Deception

1. Charles Spurgeon, *Morning and Evening* (Peabody, Mass.: Hendrickson, 1991), 392.

2. "Teen Firefighter Sets Fire at Church to Be 'Hero,'" *Associated Press*, October 24, 2007, http://www.foxnews.com/home.

3. "Miami Church Brands Members with '666' Tattoos," *Associated Press*, February 24, 2007, http://www.foxnews.com/story.

4. Matt Richtel, "Thou Shalt Not Kill, Except in a Game at Church," *New York Times*, October 7, 2007.

5. A. W. Tozer, "Self Deception and How to Avoid It," under *Christian Reader*'s article index online at http://www.Hwy777.com.

6. Ray Yungen, *A Time of Departing* (Silverton, Ore.: Lighthouse Trails, 2002, 2006), 109.

Chapter 10: Lord, Help Me Find Balance

1. Richard Exley, *The Rhythm of Life* (Tulsa: Honor Books, 1987), 149.

2. Harold Kushner, *When All You've Ever Wanted Isn't Enough* (New York: Summit Books, 1986), 57.

3. Exley, *Rhythm of Life*, 108.

4. Hayford, *The Key to Everything*, 104.

5. Adapted and expanded from a printerview found at http://www.familydoctor.org/online/famdocen/home/common/stress.

6. Tim Hansel, *When I Relax I Feel Guilty* (Chicago: David C. Cook, 1979), 30, 57.

Chapter 11: Staying Free

1. Paula Sandford, *Healing Women's Emotions* (Tulsa: Victory House, 1992), 36.

2. Adapted from John White, *Changing on the Inside* (Ann Arbor: Servant, 1991), 156–76.

Books by the Authors

By Quin Sherrer and Ruthanne Garlock

Lord, Help Me Break This Habit

Lord, I Need to Pray with Power

Lord, I Need Your Healing Power

Grandma, I Need Your Prayers

The Beginner's Guide to Receiving the Holy Spirit

Becoming a Spirit-Led Mom

God Be with Us: A Daily Guide to Praying for Our Nation (finalist for 2002 Gold Medallion Award—devotional category)

Prayer Partnerships

Praying Prodigals Home

The Making of a Spiritual Warrior

Prayers Women Pray

How to Pray for Your Children (revised edition)

A Woman's Guide to Getting Through Tough Times

A Woman's Guide to Spirit-Filled Living

A Woman's Guide to Breaking Bondages
The Spiritual Warrior's Prayer Guide
A Woman's Guide to Spiritual Warfare
How to Pray for Family and Friends
How to Forgive Your Children

Books by Quin Sherrer

Prayers from a Grandmother's Heart
Miracles Happen When You Pray
Listen, God Is Speaking to You
The Warm and Welcome Home
Good Night, Lord
A House of Many Blessings (with Laura Watson)
How to Pray for Your Children

Books by Ruthanne Garlock

Before We Kill and Eat You (with H. B. Garlock)
Fire in His Bones

Bibles Contributed to by Quin Sherrer and Ruthanne Garlock

Grandmother's Bible (Zondervan, 2008)
Women of Destiny Bible (Thomas Nelson, 2000)

About the Authors

Quin Sherrer has written or co-authored 28 books, primarily with Ruthanne Garlock, including bestsellers *A Woman's Guide to Spiritual Warfare, How to Pray for Your Children* and *Miracles Happen When You Pray.* Their book *God Be with Us: A Daily Guide to Praying for Our Nation* was nominated for the 2002 Gold Medallion Award in the devotional category by the Evangelical Christian Publishers Association.

Quin has spoken hope to audiences in forty states and twelve nations, encouraging them in their daily and sometimes challenging walks of faith. Her longtime passion has been to help others reach their God-intended purpose by sharing with them practical, biblical and sometimes humorous insights she has gained from her personal experiences and from the hundreds of people she has interviewed.

As a guest on more than three hundred radio and television programs—including *The 700 Club*, Daystar, Trinity Broadcasting Network and *100 Huntley Street*—she has addressed the topics of prayer, hospitality, miracles and personal renewal.

For a number of years, Quin served on both the U.S. national and the international board of directors for Women's Aglow Fellowship, traveling and speaking extensively in that capacity. Today she serves on the leadership team of the Northwest Florida Area Aglow.

Quin holds a B.S. degree in journalism from Florida State University. She spent her early career writing for newspapers and magazines in the Cape Kennedy, Florida, area where her husband, LeRoy, was a NASA engineer. Eight of her titles have been released through book clubs, and many of her books are available in other languages. A winner of *Guideposts* magazine's writing contest, she was also named Writer of the Year at the Florida Writers in Touch Conference.

You will not be around Quin long before you hear about her dearest friend, Jesus, her three children, her six grandchildren and her prayer partners who call themselves The Keepers. Quin often speaks to church groups, weekend seminars, Sunday congregations, professional groups and on U.S. military bases. She would be glad to have you contact her at www.quinsherrer.com or by writing to:

Quin Sherrer
P.O. Box 1661
Niceville, FL 32588

Ruthanne Garlock is a Bible teacher and author with a varied background in international ministry that crosses denominational lines. She has co-authored nineteen books with Quin Sherrer on prayer and related subjects, and often teaches on prayer and spiritual warfare for seminars and retreats. *A Woman's Guide to Spiritual Warfare* is their bestselling title.

Ruthanne also worked as senior editor for the abridged edition of *The Christian in Complete Armour*, vols. 1–3, a seventeenth-century Puritan classic by William Gurnall that has been in print for more than 350 years.

For four years she and her husband, John, served with Continental Theological Seminary in Brussels, Belgium, where they taught students from Europe and the Middle East. Then for twenty-three years they lived in Dallas, where John was an instructor at Christ For The Nations Institute and Ruthanne worked as a freelance writer and teacher. Together they traveled and taught leadership training seminars throughout the U.S. and in more than 35 countries.

Since John's sudden death in December 2003, Ruthanne is continuing the work of Garlock Ministries through her teaching and writing. She distributes John's materials in various languages for use in leadership training in many of the countries where they ministered.

Ruthanne holds a degree in Bible and religious education from Central Bible College, Springfield, Missouri, and is ordained with World Ministry Fellowship, Plano, Texas. She is on the board of elders at the Tree of Life Church, New Braunfels, Texas, and serves on the board of Christian Haitian Outreach, an orphanage ministry in Haiti. She has three adult children and four grandchildren.

Ruthanne is passionate about teaching the principles of prayer and spiritual warfare, and also about helping to equip leaders in the Third World who have limited access to training, so that they can fulfill the Great Commission through reaching their own people.

Now living in the Texas Hill Country near San Antonio, Ruthanne continues to enjoy writing, meeting with her prayer partners and traveling and teaching as God opens doors of opportunity. You may contact her at www.garlockministries. org or by writing to:

Ruthanne Garlock
P.O. Box 53
Bulverde, TX 78163